H5

£6.50

FELLOW TRAVELLERS

FELLOW TRAVELLERS

A Memoir of the Thirties

by

T. C. WORSLEY

LONDON MAGAZINE EDITIONS

First published in Great Britain 1971
by London Magazine Editions
30, Thurloe Place, S.W.7

© *1971 T. C. Worsley*

SBN 900626 69 0

Printed in Great Britain by
Billing & Sons Limited
Guildford and London

For TERENCE RATTIGAN
who also in his time chanted Arms for Spain,
with admiration and affection.

AUTHOR'S NOTE

This is not a novel, it is a memoir, fictionalised only in the sense that I have fused people involved into my characters; while the events and happenings, though they actually occurred, have been rearranged and reattributed to suit my pattern.   ·

T. C. W.

The journey is false;
the false journey is really an illness.

W. H. AUDEN

Journey to a War

INTRODUCTION

Just before the war broke out I was putting together some material I had collected into a novel about the Thirties and Spain and some of the people I knew who were caught up in that maelstrom. There were to be five main characters, all founded on real people whom those who were alive and around at the time may still vaguely remember. Martin Murray, the well-known young novelist, was then just thirty, but already on the strength of four books he had established himself as the representative figure of his generation. He was for us what someone like John Osborne was a few years ago to the young of the Fifties.

He—or someone like him—was to have been one of the main characters, and one of the threads of the novel was to have been his relationship with Harry Watson, an engaging young man who had been 'bought out' of the Scots Guards and was living in a rather uneasy domesticity with Martin at the time.

Another main character was Lady Nellie—Lady Esmerelda Griffiths. She may be remembered because she was, like the Duchess of Atholl and the Red Dean, a valuable counter in the propaganda game which the Communists were playing at the time. Her joining the Party was a ten-day wonder, for her brother, the Earl, was at the time an Under-Secretary of State for the Home Office in the National Government.

Her young nephew, Pugh, to whom she was devoted, also achieved a certain notoriety when he joined the International Brigade, and his subsequent death made its headlines in the papers—'Earl's son shot in Spain'.

Finally there was Gavin Blair Summers, a clever young

man up at Oxford, who was typical of the times in rather a different way. He was in no sense an ideologue. If he was intellectually on the Left, he was also intellectually sterile. He believed in nothing, least of all himself.

What these five characters all had in common was that they all landed up in Spain during the war in various capacities, and it was to be one aim of my novel to trace the pattern which landed each of them there.

The war interrupted my novel, but perhaps it would never have been finished in any case. I had chosen as my characters people who were too close to me just then, too real to be transferred into fiction. But that didn't strike me at the time. There was a theory going round in the Thirties that novels should be made up from careful and accurate documentation, that the first task of the novelist was to collect his documentary material and proceed from there.

I had been collecting this material for some time. I had a number of letters and diaries. I had an uncompleted novel of Gavin's, and I had supplemented these with a whole series of 'interviews' with the people themselves over the years, in which I tried to discover what they were thinking about themselves or each other, or I got from them accounts of incidents or episodes typical as I thought of the time, and I hoped that all this material would eventually coalesce into a novel. It's easy to see now the deficiencies in this method of going about things, but at the time it was very much *au movement* to work in this way. When I had it all collected it made quite a substantial pile. It looked like a real job of work, and with my 'documentary material' heaped up on a table beside me, I felt like a professional novelist in the Zolaesque tradition.

It was part of the theory that one should oneself be faceless, an anonymous editor so to speak, without bias and without individuality. 'I was a tape recorder'. So the art was to keep completely in the background and let the characters speak for themselves. Their voices alone would do the trick.

Re-reading this material lately it struck me that it might—with a few editorial notes—give an interesting slant on the Thirties, a period which I find the younger generation are now once more becoming interested in. For it has one particular resemblance to the present in that we who were young at the time were very conscious of living under the shadow of a war we knew was coming, just as the present generation are conscious of living under the shadow of the Bomb.

Our reactions were quite different from theirs, and this collection of material well illustrates what the difference was. Not that the political attitudes were all-absorbing then any more than now. Whether one lives under the shadow of a war or a Bomb, personal life is still a preoccupation for most of us: and it was so for these characters, too. But while their political reaction was typical of the times, their personal lives were not: they were exceptional in one special sense. But I offer them in the hope that they may be of some interest to those who wonder how we reacted when we were young to a not dissimilar situation.

PART ONE

The Participants

I

LADY NELLIE

Author's Note

I well remember the first of those interviews I took down. It was about Lady Nellie and was given me by Harry, who was devoted to her. I had sought Harry out at the Pleiades Bookshop, where one could usually find him of a morning. The Pleiades Bookshop—or just the Bookshop, as we called it—was on the edge of Bloomsbury. It was run by a kindly dedicated male spinster, Edmund Gladstone, who had stocked it with the powder and shot of every revolutionary movement and splinter group of the period, and it had become a kind of haven, or club, for young intellectuals, poets, artists, left-wing students and Bohemian lay-abouts. Edmund couldn't have made much out of it, for more books were borrowed than bought, and he was always ready to be 'touched' for the price of a drink, a meal or a packet of cigarettes by his young clientèle. He must, like so many middle-class people in those days, have had a small private income, and he was very generous with it. He lived above the shop, and it was he who provided refuge for those run-aways from Public Schools who were a feature of the period; and it was from the Bookshop that their anti-Public School, anti-war magazine, *Out of Bounds*, was published and distributed.

Opposite the shop was one of those grubby working-class cafés with oil-clothed tables, each with its soiled sauce-bottle on it, and a tea-urn at the counter alongside some fly-blown pies. This was all the more popular with the clientèle for being both working-class and grubby. In those days anything working-class was 'in' with the left-wing intelligentsia, while actually to be working-class like Harry, for instance, was already to be something special.

I found Harry, I remember, in the café, drinking tea with a run-away schoolboy and gossiping away in his high light voice. You wouldn't have put Harry down as an ex-guardsman to look at him. There was nothing lumpy, heavy or coarse about him. He must have fitted only to a millimetre the physical requirements of the Guards. But no amount of square-bashing had bashed out of him the lightness and ease with which he carried himself. In a room he always seemed to be half dancing, and even when sitting down his eyes danced. They were so lively, so vivacious, so full of the pleasure of the immediate moment. With his jet black hair and sloe eyes he was undeniably attractive.

Then, too, he was one of the most adaptable young men you have ever met. His capacity to fit himself into any situation or social circumstances was remarkable in one who had after all come from a miner's terrace. It was this capacity which had served him so well when he first burst upon London and discovered that there were plenty of willing gentlemen ready to play host to such an engaging personality. Where his companions might be equally sought after for grosser reasons, Harry was welcome because he fitted in to whatever occasion arose. He was very 'presentable'; he could be presented even to the respectable. He could be taken to a smart restaurant or a grand hotel and instinctively knew how to behave.

So already, before Martin Murray arrived in his life, he was a social as well as a sexual success in that area of London where Guardsmen plied their civilian trade. He had been 'bought out' by an earlier admirer and had already, with him, visited Paris, Venice, the South of France. But his special quality was that he was at home anywhere, as much at home in this grubby workman's café as in the Ivy or the Café de Paris.

16

His association with Martin had already lasted three years. It had been a case of instant attraction between them, and Harry had very much seen himself as the companion to a writer, especially a writer who made frequent trips abroad. He acquired a typewriter and taught himself a form of typing which more or less passed muster. He would be a secretary-companion. He saw himself answering important letters and meeting interesting people. He would make himself a life out of it. And if it hadn't worked out quite like that, he was not disposed to blame himself over it.

Martin was inevitably very Left-wing, and Harry himself had soon assimilated all the Left-wing attitudes and picked up all the Left-wing phrases. But he had just lately gone further than that. He had been flirting with the Party and was just about ready to join it. It seemed to the others, at least to Martin and certainly to Gavin, an odd decision. The puritanism and discipline which characterised the Party's outlook on life seemed somehow alien to this pleasure-loving evanescent personality. But no doubt, they thought, he would find a way of fitting himself into it, as he fitted in everywhere else; and meanwhile, away from the Party, he was still the easy, lackadaisical character he had always been.

I would probably have suggested we had lunch together at Bertorelli's, the little Italian restaurant in Charlotte Street where in those days you could get a satisfying meal at a ridiculously cheap price. Harry would readily have agreed: he always agreed to everything, and over the spaghetti I evidently got him talking, as planned, about Lady Nellie. This is the record I have of that conversation:

She's a heavenly woman, Harry said. We gossip together for hours on end; she's very understanding. If I have a row with Martin—and I'm often having rows with Martin now —I always fly round to her, and she'll always listen, and take me out to dinner and cheer me up. Of course she's very serious about things, too, and so should we all be. But she loves a bit of gossip, that's the great thing about her. I do sometimes get rather bored with the intensity of people like Martin, you see. They never let up. But with Nellie you can let your hair down and have a good old natter. And she isn't stuck up at all, you know. Not a bit.

'How did you come to meet her?'

At Martin's. She came there quite a lot. One day we had a long talk when Martin was out, and I realised how lonely she was. You see she's a passionate Socialist and with this posh family of hers, she finds it very difficult. Her brother David, the present Earl, is an Under-Secretary or something in the National Government—just an ordinary conventional ruling-class figure—and her late husband the Colonel was very stuffy, too. So she's had no one to talk to about it all. So I said I'd introduce her to the Bookshop crowd and I did. She doesn't live very far away. So when I was up there one day and there was no one around to gossip with, I went and called on her.

She lives in a rather dowdy square actually; she made the Colonel move—that's when he was alive. She couldn't bear S.W.3 where all her relations and their friends live, and the Colonel, who adored her, gave in though he was much happier in S.W.3 himself.

Anyhow, there she is quite near the Bookshop and I knew there were lots of people there she'd like. And I took her round and introduced her to Edmund who runs it, and of course it was just her cup of tea. You know what the Bookshop crowd are like. Well, she'd never seen anything like it. After her stuffy relations, those poets and intellectuals were just what she was looking for. And some of them are always dropping in every day, aren't they? You can always find someone sympathetic to talk to round the Bookshop. And though Edmund does his best to help them out when he can, he isn't rich like Nellie is, and can't manage very much. But she was always good for a pound or two or was ready to take any of us round to Percy Street for a meal now and then. It's quite transformed her life, she says. It's funny how someone like her could be so lonely before, isn't it? She says the only people she could talk to were in the Ethical Society which was where she began her revolt. You see it was over Catholicism that it started with her. All her family were Catholics, and the Colonel, too. And her first struggle was against Catholicism. She's still a bit caught up in all that, because her family are so intense about it.

What I tell her is that she ought to join the Communist Party. She'd find lots of friends there. She's thinking about it. She couldn't while the Colonel was alive. He put his foot down over that. She said that as she became more and more Socialist she had wanted to drop her title. But the Colonel wouldn't hear of it.

She's very funny about her name. It's really Esmerelda: and she never stops blaming her mother for giving her such a silly name. But she wouldn't call herself Lady Esmerelda, and Lady Nellie, she says, sounds like a typical frivolous Twenties character. She's very funny about herself, Nellie is. She's funny about the late Colonel, too. She says whatever ideas anyone has about Colonels were embodied in her Jonathan. But she has to admit that he was really very nice. Because he was. But that's the point, she says. Among the ideas embodied in a Colonel are some very good qualities—loyalty, honourableness, truthfulness. But what was the good of loyalty in a man who admired Stanley Baldwin and thought Hitler was probably right about the Jews? Or what was the good of truthfulness in a man who believed in the infallibility of the Pope? That's the sort of thing she says.

'Have you met her brother, David, the Earl?'

I did once, yes. He seems all right really. Just what you'd expect. Very la-di-da and posh but quite gentle with it. And you can understand that when she tells you about their childhood. Apparently the father was a very strong man, very coarse and violent. So she says, anyway, and he frightened her brother out of his wits as a boy. He was very feeble then, a bed-wetter, she says, and she had to fight to protect him from the Old Man. But then when the Old Man died of a heart attack when David was eighteen, David blossomed. He slowly turned into what his father had wanted and what Nellie calls an upper-class dummy. She watched the process with fury. He'd been to Public School and was already what she calls a first generation gentleman. He went from there into the Guards and became a pukka Guardee.

Well, you know what those Guards officers are like! I do, anyhow. Terrifically superior and stuck-up. And when he came out, he became head of the business and had a real flare for it. So there he is now—all the things she hates, and has quite forgotten he was ever anything else. So I can see how it infuriates her, can't you? And her mother infuriates her even more. Because when the Old Man was alive, he apparently treated her like dirt, and she had a perfectly miserable life, snubbed all the time like a poor relation. But now she's blossomed, too. Nellie took me to see her once. I thought she was an old duck.

She sits there in a great brocaded chair presiding over The Family as if she were a great Matriach in some film with thousand of descendants, when there aren't really very many. But that's all right. It's a game she plays, and it does no one any harm, but it infuriates Nellie. I don't see why. But there's no telling with families, is there? Nellie took me there to lunch. Between you and I, I think she wanted to shock the Old Lady by introducing as a friend of hers someone who was definitely working-class. But the Old Lady didn't bat an eyelid.

As a matter of fact we got on like a house on fire. We had a common interest in private-eye detective stories—Raymond Chandler and all those. I promised to send her a Hank Jansen. She'd never heard of him. But she wouldn't be shocked. She's one of those grand old ladies who's beyond shocking.

But all this maddened Nellie. It seems that when the old man, the first Earl, was alive, her mother read nothing but Henry James and Flaubert in the original. She had a terrible life, according to Nellie. He was a common old brute and beastly to her, and her line was Yeats and helping the local theatre and admiring the pre-Raphaelites and being squashed for it. Then as soon as he died, she changed. She gave up all her poetry and that, reads nothing but these detective stories and talks about the Bon Dieu as if He were an old acquaintance. I say good luck to her after that life. But Nellie goads her and goads her, with Socialism and everything, and the Old Lady just raises her eyes to heaven and refuses to be rattled.

You can't help seeing that it's tough for Nellie, the family being so posh and all that, and they do behave just like caricatures. They really are shocked by any reference to Socialism. They consider it 'bad form', as if that had anything to do with it.

Nellie wants us to take care of this nephew of hers, Pugh —he's a step-nephew, actually—when he comes to stay for some of his holidays with her. She's very keen on him, and thinks that if he gets in with our crowd it'll do him the world of good. He's at this Catholic school, which sounds awful, but has given up Catholicism and she thinks he's just ripe for Socialism. She has lots of photos of him and I must say he looks a dream. I'm quite ready to take him up, when he comes.

'Is she a Marxist?' I asked him.

Well, she is in a way. But she's still hesitating about joining the Party. She's read all the books and knows the theory thoroughly. That's a funny thing about her, considering her background and everything, how she has this passion for reading and studying. She has Marx and Engels and all of them, and great note-books in which she makes notes and commentaries on it all. Yet she isn't heavy about it, if you see what I mean.

She's really very extraordinary, Nellie, I adore her.

Author's Note

Such, then, was the first entry in my file, scrupulously marked 'Lady Nellie'. I didn't at this time know her very intimately and much of the information was new to me. I had met her several times and what had struck me was the contradictions between her character and her appearance. She was always playing down her family as being vulgar *nouveau riche*, and yet she had this typically aristocratic appearance, the height, the elongated, delicate bonework in the face. Her manner, too, had that absolute assurance that is typical of the well-born. She was only forty but her hair had gone quite white. This didn't make her look old because with it she had a marvellous complexion, a sort of luminosity of the skin from within. Altogether she was a most striking-looking person.

And then, at odds with that, was the passion with which she blasted out her Socialist convictions all over the place. And it wasn't a question of trying to shock. She really couldn't bear to be silent when pompous people on social occasions referred, say, to the unemployed as unemployables or said, which the middle-classes were always saying at this time, that they could find work if they wanted—they preferred living on the dole. Or people would, as they frequently did in her circle, say that there was much to be said for Hitler. He was cleaning the country up, had put an end to strikes, was getting rid of all those Socialists and Intellectuals. On such occasions Lady Nellie simply couldn't keep quiet and burst out at them in a fury, or simply stormed off.

Yet she was, I recall, a decidedly incongruous figure among the sloppy Bookshop crowd. But it was just these incongruities which had attracted her to me as a candidate for one of my main characters, and having filed Harry's opinion of her, I evidently set about getting another one from Martin.

Martin lived in Bloomsbury, too, in an airy, tall-windowed flat in Bedford Square. Its décor was based on ideas he had come across in Vienna, and it looked resolutely and rather uncomfortably modern, with Swedish plain wood furniture, lights reflected from the ceiling, chairs that looked like inverted mushrooms, and semi-abstract pictures on the walls. All this was sufficiently unusual at this time to give the journalists and gossip-writers just the right revolutionary image with which to start their paragraphs.

What was most striking about Martin was his long, thin, sensitive, suffering face. The suffering was internal—his circumstances, enough money, and a remarkable talent, were easy enough on the surface. But he agonised for the world. He had been in Germany during the worst of the Nazi terror and had seen friends and acquaintances, Socialists, Jews, Intellectuals, hounded out of the country or herded into concentration camps. He had seen the burning of the books: he had heard the tramp of feet up the stairs and the knock on the door in the night. Thus he felt in himself a peculiar responsibility to be active on political platforms when his natural inclination was for travel and for writing. Over this he was in constant conflict with himself.

But, then, just in general he was in constant conflict with himself. I often think of him as having combined in his remarkable person about as many of the current neuroses as could easily be fitted into one man. But whereas these, in a less extraordinary personality, would surely in the end have produced a breakdown, if not a madness, he was somehow able to contain them. He had a remarkable capacity for enduring contradictions, and never minded being caught out in them. They frequently exposed themselves in him because he was an exceptionally, almost unnaturally, candid man. He had a way of blurting out the truth wherever he happened to be or whoever he happened to be with, irrespective of whether it might wound, discomfort or embarrass.

It was, of course, only the truth, as he saw it at that moment. At another moment he might see it quite differently, and then, if he did, he would blurt that out, too. And he no more thought of the embarrassment to himself of the contradiction than he thought of the embarrassment to others of some candid judgement or remark.

In spite of the attention he attracted in the press and elsewhere, he was never the least pompous. Or rather if he ever caught himself being so, he was the first to giggle and withdraw.

His view of Lady Nellie at this time is the second item in her file:

Nellie is really rather extraordinary, Martin said. One can't help admiring the distance she's come on her own, and with that family background to contend with. I don't really quite see where her passion of revolt comes from. I suppose if one could trace it back, one would find its origins in a really violent father-fixation. Her mother, you see, was this refined, well-bred, cultivated, probably rather ineffectual woman, while the father was coarse-fibred and tough-willed and had only married her, one supposes, for the social prestige she brought with her—she was apparently a duke's second cousin, or something of the sort.

Nellie, one imagines, inherited some of her father's toughness and fighting spirit, but identified herself passionately with the down-trodden mother, and fought the father tooth and nail, fighting on behalf of both her mother and her rather feeble brother, too.

Then when the father died, and the fight was over, both brother and mother as it were betrayed her.

So now poor Nellie's passion of revolt is turned against these two and what they stand for. That's how I seem to see it. And it's certainly true that you can't appreciate Nellie unless you can see her still caught in some passionate family struggle. The odd thing is that for all her intelligence—and she has her own kind of intelligence—she can't somehow see this for herself. She can't distance herself enough from the family to see that all her political passion, for instance, isn't political at all really—at the roots. It's neurotic, of course, and this is what gives her arguments a sort of total unreality even when they are logically right and theoreti-lly valid.

The fact is that she's really a B.F., by which I mean (on the analogy of B.C.) that she's Before Freud, and that gulf is totally unbridgeable. She gave me once a really horrifying account of her marriage. She married only to get away from home, and she wasn't in love with her husband. In fact she didn't really know what being in love meant physically. She had had a wild schoolgirl attachment for a romantically handsome elder boy cousin, who had 'loved' her platonically like a knight in a story: and she had adored that. It went on for two or three years, before he disappeared and married someone else. Then this Jonathan, the Colonel, who had always been waiting in the background, proposed to her.

She had been devastated by the 'treachery' of the cousin's desertion of her, and Jonathan had a lot to recommend him. He was almost part of the family (you see the pattern!). He was kind and good and gentle, loved her deeply, and was thoroughly acceptable. So she accepted him.

But she accepted him without knowing in the least what marriage meant. No one had told her anything. No one had prepared her for the wedding night. You know how sometimes she gets girlish and skittish? Well, she was like that with her new husband. She was still playing the little girl. While he was undressing, tactfully in the bathroom, she hid in a big wardrobe cupboard, meaning to jump out and give him a fright. When he came in ready for the fray, she was horrified.

She's quite funny about it. She had evidently got over it in a sort of way. Having a streak of rationality, she isn't revolted by sex, as she might well have been. She just thinks it doesn't matter one way or the other.

This makes her very sympathetic in one sense—for instance, she's awfully sweet with Harry, she takes him out when he's feeling down, and lets him talk for hours about how badly I treat him! But the thing is that she doesn't really understand either about him and me, or about herself. Her own lack of sexuality leaves her somehow hung up—out of life in some way.

26

'Gavin always calls her that ghastly woman.'

That's rubbish. She's not ghastly at all. She's silly, pretty often, but that's all right. It's her curious, isolated, passionate and blinkered politics that baffle me. Within the narrow limits of her thinking, she is extraordinarily logical, and drives her arguments to their very end. She would have murdered Robespierre, and would gladly kill Hitler if she could get at him.

But she somehow can't relate in any way to the real world. And being very rich makes this possible. Herself and her political passion are somehow at total odds, so that she floats through life on two quite separate planes. It's that, fundamentally, that makes her seem silly. And the fact that her passion is for all the things we regard as right and desirable doesn't really make it either more sensible or more real.

So you have this odd phenonemon of a rich, kind, amusing, yesterday's B.F. woman sucked into today by this psychotic drive. I really wonder sometimes how she will survive its pull, whether it won't tear her apart if something doesn't happen. Meanwhile she's also rather wonderful. It may be easy for her to give so much money to helping Jews escape from the Nazis, which she does, but most people don't; and she is very prepared to do much more about it than just give money—only no one would trust her in action. I mean, she's one of the most absurdly impractical people I've ever met. And she rather annoyingly plays on that a bit. Still, she's a wonderfully generous-hearted person and one day if the two halves of her come together, she might be a real force.

'But she is serious about politics, surely?'

Oh yes, she's serious in her own way. She reads it all up and she knows all the slogans and catchwords. She can use phrases like 'the dictatorship of the proletariat', 'monopoly capitalism', 'exploitation of the workers', 'nationalisation of the means of production', and all that. But it's all theory to her. The thing is, you see, that like everyone else who has had to educate themselves, it's all in her head, and suddenly finding herself among like-minded people, she's in a fever to argue things out with them, and see how her theories stand up. So all she really wants is to engage in long theoretical arguments which I find boring. But now Harry's introduced her to the Bookshop crowd, I dare say she'll find willing listeners enough. You know what they're like there. For the price of a lunch they'd listen to anyone.

Harry, too, may help her there. His view of politics is almost wholly practical, and he'll probably draw her in to joining the Party where she can combine theory with action. Or so she'll suppose. But I don't expect it will work out quite so simply as that. The Communists in action are very different from the Communists in theory, as she'll soon find out. They'll use her for what they can get out of her, and when she discovers they're doing that she won't like it. That's what I mean by it all being in her head. She knows the theory all right. But she has yet to come up against the Party in practice and it isn't the same thing.

'So you think she'll end by joining the Party?'

I rather fear so. After all, she was brought up as an ardent Catholic and all her family still are. But having been a Catholic she won't find the Party orthodoxy as difficult to swallow as, say, I would. Orthodoxy is in her intellectual blood, so to speak. She may well be searching around for a new one to take the place of the old, feeling perhaps a little lost without some strait-jacket of belief to contain her. And the Communists will supply that all right! But my point is that people like her who have hardly experienced freedom don't find that strait-jacket so constricting as those who have not only experienced freedom, but simply can't do without it, like me.

Gavin's contributions were always the easiest of all to obtain. There was nothing he welcomed so warmly as an interruption of any kind. For he commonly spent his mornings in the vacations from Oxford downstairs in the sitting-room of his mother's tiny house in Bayswater. There he would sit, as he often told me, staring dully at the 'set-books' which he was supposed to be reading for his Oxford degree, and finding no possible reason to convince himself that they were worth studying. Or, worn out after an hour of this sterile exercise, he would get out his typewriter and set it up, determined to add another page to the autobiographical novel he was writing. But when the paper was in place and all was ready, he would sit motionless again staring dully this time at that blank page and finding nothing, absolutely nothing, to put on it. How could he write a novel about himself, he would complain, when absolutely nothing happened to him?

Gavin's dissatisfaction was bottomless, and he spent a good deal of his energy and his undoubted intelligence in defending it if you tried to take it away. It was somehow necessary to him. Perhaps it was in some way an unresolved aspect of the running warfare which he kept up with his mother.

His mother, who lay upstairs all morning in her bedroom, adored him and, though she was upstairs, she was never out of touch. Or so he used to claim. If he picked up the telephone, he could always hear her picking up the extension and shamelessly listening in to his conversation. If he made a move to go out, she instantly heard and called down to him, where was he going, who was he going with, when could she expect him back, would he be in to lunch, tea, dinner?

The one asset he might have claimed to have got from her was his good looks. But his dissatisfaction extended even to them. Instead of accepting that he was a very nice-looking boy, he picked on the smallness of his mouth, the comparative shortness of his eyelashes and above all his lack of height. He was decidedly on the small side. No one could deny that anyhow.

Yet quite contradicting all this, he also had a great share of his mother's vivacity and brought to his most pessimistic diagnoses of himself and his state an amused and amusing power of analysis. It was this which, in spite of his nihilism, made him great fun to be with. He was destructive about everybody as well as himself. His family was what was called well-connected, and he had as an uncle, the husband of his mother's sister, a well-known ex-diplomat of the time, Sir George Anchor, a passionate Liberal, whose last book, warning of the danger of war from Nazism, had made a great stir, especially on the Left. He and his mother went down to Sir George's place fairly regularly, so that Gavin was rather more in the social swim than we were.

His contribution is the next in Nellie's file:

NELLIE'S FILE III

Why do you bother about her, Gavin said. She's just slightly mad. She goes to Shaw Wood a lot, you know, where my uncle Sir George lives, and she's always holding forth in a muddled sort of way. She's a passionate Socialist and anti-Catholic. She has some sort of obsession that all the troubles of the world come from the Catholics.

'How does your Uncle George treat her?'

Tolerantly, as he treats everyone. And that's even worse. He takes her arguments quite seriously and tries to show her the illogicalities, and that encourages her to go on and on. Argument for her is like drink for some people. Once started, she can't stop. And she goes round and round and round in some obsessive circle inside her head. As for arguing logically with her, it's out of the question. There's no logic in anything she says.

'But surely you're more in sympathy with her than with your uncle?'

It isn't as simple as that. You see, Sir George is a good man. He really is. And he really is tolerant. I suppose he's a real Liberal, not a bogus one. He really does believe in everyone being allowed their own opinions. And if that's so, the Catholics are entitled to theirs. And when he says that, Lady Nellie thumps away like a drum and works herself into a passion.

'Everyone else talks about her as being "such fun". Don't you find that at all?'

Not really, you know, I don't. I seem to remember she was when we were children. She was rather good at playing all sorts of games, and I seem to remember her laughing a lot, and everyone else laughing with her, but I never liked games.

'Have you been to their place in Monmouth?'

Yes, we had a weekend there, not so long ago.

'What's it like?'

It's a marvellous house. One of those long, low, white tall-windowed Regency places with lovely rooms, but rather hideously furnished and filled with those ghastly Academy pictures—not the funny anecdotal ones—Edwardian Greek girls in floating dresses, that sort of thing, 'collected' by her father. And then David Griffiths is rather a pomp. Quite a nice pomp actually, and Nellie never stops badgering them about how awful they are, as a family, *nouveau riche* and vulgar and all that.

'Well, they are actually, aren't they?'

You wouldn't know it now. Apparently the father was—well, you can see it from those terrible pictures. His own

31

father had built up quite a big shipping business in Cardiff before the Great War and then, of course, when the war started and shipping was at a premium they became millionaires or multi-millionaires. This father of hers was now the head of the business and went into Lloyd George's government and first bought himself a Barony and then squeezed an Earldom out of the Welsh Wizard. It was quite a scandal at the time, my uncle says. But, of course, David went to one of the best schools and you couldn't tell that they weren't always as grand as they are now. David may be a bit of a pomp but he keeps his temper rather well, considering how Nellie goes on at him. Of course, she's a wild Socialist, and is always trying to convert young Pugh.

'And he isn't convertible?'

Young Pugh? God, no. He's just a very attractive little tough who doesn't get on with his step-father. He rather hates everyone actually. But I like him. We mooched around the grounds together, and he has quite a funny way of attacking everything. You would have thought his aunt could see he wasn't the kind of boy to be interested in her politics; but once she was launched there was no stopping her. She was giving him a sort of first course in Socialism all through the weekend, and he wasn't having it.

[*Knowing how Gavin enjoyed doing his imitations, I encouraged him.*]

'How did it go?'

She'd say something like 'Take a shipwright', because she thought that would interest him. 'Take a shipwright,' she'd say. 'He puts his whole being into riveting. The ship that's finally built is the product of the collective guts, blood, sinews, muscle, skill of all those shipwrights. Yet does the boat belong to them, as it should by rights when they'd finished? No, it belongs to strangers, to the outsiders who had contributed nothing but the capital.' 'But that's us!' objected young Pugh indignantly, 'We supply the

32

capital.' 'But, don't you see, it isn't fair,' Lady Nellie would try and explain. 'We haven't done anything to create that ship directly. It ought to belong to those who made it with their hands and their skill.'

Pugh, of course, wouldn't see it. 'We don't provide only the capital. We supply all the organisation and the shipyard, too.'

'But the shipyard oughtn't to be *ours*: it ought to be *theirs*.'

'But it *is* ours.'

'Don't you see it isn't fair? We ought to hand them over.'

Pugh didn't see: 'What would happen to us then?'

'We'd have our share and no more. We'd be just like them.'

'Thank you very much!' young Pugh said, laughing at her. But she wouldn't see that he was hopeless material for her. And on she went, all through dinner, too.

'Look at coal!' she'd suddenly say. 'Suppose the coal-mines were nationalised. The coal would belong to us, the community. It's a national asset. It oughtn't to be in private hands.'

'Oh, drop it, Nellie,' her brother said.

But Pugh was enjoying himself.

'Why not, Aunt Nellie?'

'Because the owners can't use it properly. They aren't interested in coal; they're only interested in profits.'

'And the men are only interested in wages,' Pugh argued.

'Yes and rightly as long as they don't own what they produce. But if you nationalised the mines, the miners would own their own produce, and there'd be no more strikes.'

'Well, I could stop strikes in a moment,' Pugh said.

'How?'

'By shooting all the strikers,' and he enjoyably made the noise of a machine gun.

B   33

That was the sort of conversation she kept up all the weekend. She simply couldn't keep off it.

The next day at lunch she was on at her brother, David, about a planned economy. 'Think of all the effort put into making hundreds of different lines of shoes, for example. Some lines go and some lines don't, and all those that don't are wasted.'

And it didn't matter what you did, whether you changed the subject or continued the argument, she was equally passionate.

When David quite reasonably answered the shoe argument by saying 'And who will decide which are the best lines to develop before the consumer has had a chance of deciding by choice?', instead of following the argument on, she flew into a temper and said she wasn't being taken seriously.

No, Nellie is hell!

'She does a lot of good work, doesn't she?'

Does she? I don't know. I suppose she may. They're stinking rich, you know, so if she hands out a few free dinners and pound notes to the Bookshop crowd, she can well afford it. Besides, that's only buying herself in, really. They put up with her for the dinners and the pound notes, I should imagine. She spends a lot of time there now because, of course, they'll all talk politics, too, by the hour. But they must see what a muddle-head she is. She's a real romantic, Nellie. She hasn't any idea how the world really works. She lives in a day-dream where everyone is equal and everyone loves everyone. But then she never has to worry about anything real. She's well above it all. She irritates me talking all that sort of guff without knowing what it really entails. She isn't real somehow, though who am I to talk?

34

NELLIE'S FILE IV

[*The next item in Nellie's file explains itself. I happened to have met Nellie and Harry just after they had been involved in a nasty fracas with Mosley's bully boys, and they were full of it.*]

'It was terrible, quite terrible,' Nellie said. 'I saw the whole thing at close quarters. I'd arranged to go to this meeting with Harry: it was just a perfectly peaceful meeting organised by the Communists for a protest against the Government arms policy. Well, I was rather late . . .'

'As you always are,' said Harry indulgently.

'This time I really couldn't help it. I even took a taxi.'

'As you always do,' said Harry, gently mocking her. 'It's her feet,' he explained to me. 'She will wear these high heels, won't you, ducks, and she can't walk in them. So you take a taxi to the meetings and leave it round the corner, so you won't be seen by the comrades.'

'They're so puritan about things like that,' she agreed, but still a little hysterically, for they were both worked up. 'And I feel guilty. So I did the same thing here, got out of the taxi round the corner and walked down to Park Road. This Park Road was a cul-de-sac and the meeting was taking place at the far end of it. It was already going by the time I got there; a little group of people with their banners round the platform, and I could hear the speaker haranguing them from the very top. And then just as I turned the corner into Park Road these four green vans swirled round the corner and skidded to a halt. They were plain vans with wire over the windows, and out of each of them there jumped five young men in the uniform of Mosley's Fascists. Black shirts and grey trousers, horrible looking toughs. I was as close to them as this, and I can tell you as they jumped down they were all fitting knuckle-dusters on their fingers. Then they ran charging down the cul-de-sac, ten abreast in two lines.

'The meeting at the bottom hadn't seen them. It was a perfectly peaceful meeting, a hundred people or so, I suppose, and you know how it is at these meetings; they're partly an outing, and there were women with their children and perambulators and thermoses, leaning against the walls. And those horrible young men just bowled everything over in their path to the meeting, women, children, everyone, and then they weighed into the meeting and smashed it up.'

Harry took up the tale from there.

'We didn't know anything, you see, until they were among us. They took us completely by surprise. No one was expecting anything. They ploughed through us, knocking everyone over, upset our portable platform, smashed the banners and knocked out everyone in sight. I began running but one tripped me up and I grazed my knee really badly, look! It was all over in a moment though, before we could pick ourselves up and organise anything. Directly they'd overturned the platform and smashed the banners they were off again, leaving us dazed. Several of the comrades had bleeding noses, and one had a really nasty cut in the cheek. Those bloody knuckle-dusters! Half of us were sprawling on the ground and the rest too surprised to do anything. They just didn't care. One little boy was knocked over and was crying; and they didn't make any distinction, women or men, they knocked them all down and then they were gone again.'

'I stayed by the vans,' Nellie said. 'I was too surprised to do anything else. And after scattering the meeting they were back in next to no time. And meanwhile their vans, directly they jumped out, had been quickly reversed and turned round waiting for them; and they ran up the street and jumped in again, laughing and grinning to each other, thoroughly pleased with themselves, and were driven off.

36

'Well, I went down the cul-de-sac to see what I could do. There'd been two policemen standing watching the meeting and they'd done nothing, absolutely nothing. I know, because I'd watched them. They just stood aside and let it all happen. And now it was all over they started moving people on and clearing the street. Someone had tried to get the meeting going again, righting the platform and meaning to draw the lessons from what we'd seen, but the police wouldn't let them.'

'Nellie was marvellous,' Harry now interrupted. 'You should have heard her in her best upper-class manner demanding to know why they'd done nothing. Not that it budged them. "You just move along, Lady," they said. "It's all over now." "It's by no means over," Nellie told them. "That's the most disgraceful thing I've ever seen. This was a perfectly harmless meeting until those toughs came in. They were wearing knuckle-dusters, I saw them. I want to give evidence." But the police wouldn't have it; they just turned their backs on her and went on pushing people off.

' "You listen to me," Nellie shouted at them. "I'll take your numbers. You haven't heard the end of this." And one of them turned round getting really ugly. "Now you mind your own business and let us mind ours." "But it *is* my business," Nellie said. "It's the business of every decent citizen when these people can cause riots in a peaceful street and you do nothing about it all. I shall report you. Do you know who I am?"

"I don't care who you are," the policeman said. "If you don't move on I'll have you for obstruction."

' "I'll move on," Nellie said. "I'll move straight on to my brother, who's your Under-Secretary. We'll see what he's got to say."

' "You do that, and hurry up about it," was all the change she got out of the policeman.

'Well, it was no use arguing, that was for sure. And the meeting was over: people had picked themselves up and were dispersing and the police wouldn't let the speaker go on. So Nellie said, "Come on. That's what we'll do. We'll go and report this to David. He's bound to do something when he hears what's happened."

'But of course he wouldn't,' said Nellie. 'He'd hardly listen. He was there at the Boltons with mother presiding over the tea things. I told them what had happened and showed them Harry's knee, badly grazed. And David was at his most sniffy. "That's what comes of fighting in the streets," he said. "But we weren't fighting," I told him. "We were having a quite peaceful orderly meeting, till those thugs drove up." "If you will attend street corner meetings," he said loftily, "You must expect what you get."

'You see how it is! They don't know anything, these ruling-class dummies. They don't know how democracy was lost in Germany by the Government allowing the Nazis to break up peaceful meetings. They just don't know. They think politics is all quietly decided in the Clubs and the Houses of Parliament. They think they're the only people entitled to have politics in their smug ruling-class way. They think the workers ought to keep quiet and do what they're told. And if they fight for their rights, they're causing a disturbance and deserve all they get. The fact is that David and his lot really sympathise secretly with the Fascists. They want these meetings broken up. They want the workers kept in their place. Look at mother sitting complacently there in her lace, pouring out China tea and handing round the cucumber sandwiches, and saying that it's all the Communists' fault: if they stayed at home, they wouldn't provoke the others. What can she know about it? She's never had to go without anything all her life. But it's no use. There's no persuading David and his lot. They're armoured by their own ignorance, and their smugness too.

I could have killed David, and knocked over that silver tray and all it stood for. But what's the use?   We just left.'

[*They went on milling over the incident till it was time for us to go. I walked Harry back to his flat and asked him for his version of the meeting between Nellie and her brother.*]

'It was just as she said,' Harry told me. 'They haven't an idea, have they, and they just think Nellie is a bit potty. It's not surprising, is it really? I mean, how should they know, living like that, what really goes on? And, of course, Nellie's hopeless with them. She gets too excited and all incoherent when she's with them. As soon as we arrived, you see, she brushed the maid aside when she opened the door, and began shouting up the stairs; and she's too neurotic with them to get it all clear. She burst into the drawing-room with the tea all laid out like she said, attacking David before he knew what it was all about. "It's your police, David, they're a disgrace, they aren't doing their duty. They didn't do a thing to help, did they, Harry?" She's always like that with them, dear Nellie, beginning in the middle and with her voice on that neurotic note. David's really very nice, you know, just very blinkered and protected from it all, if you see what I mean. While he thought it might be an accident or something in which the police had behaved badly, he was very ready to listen. But when he'd calmed her down and got some of the real story out of her, he stopped being interested, like she said. I suppose there are dozens of these incidents going on all the time, and they just think it very common and badly bred to attend street meetings. Well, they never would, would they, except at elections?

'I soon saw it was no use expecting anything from David and I tried to calm Nellie down and have some tea. I must say I rather like the Old Lady sitting there so grand and we get on together, and what I say is you might as well enjoy yourselves while you can. There's something very

39

reassuring about that tea-time ritual at those houses, isn't there? The parlour-maid in her cap and uniform and all, and the silver all spread out and the sandwiches and the cakes. What impression can you possibly make on that? Much better accept it and enjoy it, I say. But, of course, Nellie couldn't. She read them a long lecture on how the Fascists and the Nazis gained control of the streets. She told them of the castor oil and the concentration camps and the beatings and the tortures, all in a terrible muddle.

'They didn't begin to understand, those two: they just thought us hysterical, and I see how it happens. Nellie doesn't though. It's all so alive to her and then she's used to all that grandeur, isn't she? It means nothing to her. She could see it swept away without turning a hair. But that's how it is, isn't it? You don't mind so much giving up what you've had. But if you haven't had it, it looks rather different.'

II

MARTIN MURRAY

Author's Note

Author's Note

I know why I decided to open Martin's file with an interview with Nellie: for I had good reason to think she knew something about his background:

MARTIN'S FILE I

Oh yes, we used to come across the Murrays. They were very rich. Paper, I think. But we didn't know them very well. They were one of the great Liberal families, friends of the Fry's and the Cadbury's, and that lot. Whereas my father was an out-and-out Tory, and David hasn't the guts to be anything else. Besides which, our being Catholics would have put the families out of sympathy. But I came across Martin's father at several house-parties just at the time I was fighting my way out of my Catholicism, and found him very sympathetic. In fact he helped me quite a lot. That's old Sir Edward, the one you can hear occasionally making very wary speeches about the dangers of Fascism. Of course, he's getting on now. He was much more advanced politically when he was younger, and was even called a 'Socialist' by other businessmen who disapproved of his Radicalism—Sir Edward, I mean. He was a great one for all his employees owning shares in the business. But I don't know that it worked out. Half measures never do, do they?

But certainly Martin would never have had the same sort of struggle we've all had to have. And there wasn't any fuss, I don't believe, when he decided not to go into the family firm, but to devote himself to writing; and they're all proud of him. That's why I think he ought to be a little more sympathetic to Harry. He's had such an easy time himself. But perhaps that's just what prevents him. He doesn't realise what a struggle it is for someone like Harry to push his way from where he's come. I understand it better, because I've had to fight every inch of the way myself, and even now it isn't easy trying to fight against David and Mother. . . .

'But Martin,' I reminded her.

Yes, well, Martin is a great influence, you know, with the young. And he's in a much more responsible position than he seems to realise. He can't really quite make the break with his Liberal past. Perhaps it isn't quite so easy for him as I said it was. Because, you see, in the end the Liberal position only lands one into supporting the ruling class, doesn't it? In some ways it's even more dangerous than plain Toryism. You know where you are with that. But the Liberals, by pretending to stand for freedom of all kinds, seem to be on our side when they're not really, not when it really comes down to it. I mean the issues are absolutely clear now, aren't they? Are you for us or against us? And the Liberals are neither. Well, Martin is really stuck half-way. I suppose with that Liberal tradition behind him, it's rather hard to break with it. They seem so reasonable. I mean, it's like Gavin's uncle, Sir George, down at Shaw Wood. Of course, he's a great friend of the Murray's. That was where I met Sir Edward. Sir George, you see, argues that if you believe in freedom, you must believe in allowing Catholics their freedom, too. And he won't see where that leads to.

Martin has obviously inherited a lot of these scruples.

42

He demands absolute freedom for himself to write 'the truth', for instance. But what is 'the truth'? Surely the truth is to be on the side of history? And if what he writes or speaks damages the working-class struggle, surely he shouldn't do it? We argue this a lot. But he can't quite throw off those last vestiges of Liberalism. And this weakens him enormously.

But he is a little weak, Martin. He's too ready to see every side of every question and that, we know, leads to paralysis. On the other hand he does marvellous work as well, you know. I mean among the refugees. I can't tell you how many he's helped to get out, and he never talks about it, or boasts. He's a very good man really, there's no doubt about that. But I do wish he could see more of Harry's side of things. When I talk to him about it, he's rather annoying, treating me as if I don't understand. When it's really him that isn't understanding. He doesn't seem to understand how fond of him Harry really is. Harry would do anything for him. He really would! But he keeps Harry at a distance, as if he was intruding. Says he interferes with his work. But I'm sure Harry doesn't. Harry's so proud of Martin's work!

Personally, I think Martin's work is a little disruptive. It's all right making fun of the ruling class who deserve it. But some of his portraits of the workers are really almost malicious. You see, as he won't join in with them, he only sees them from the outside. If he was working *with* them, I'm sure he'd find they were quite different. Or at least he'd understand why they seem as dogmatic as they do. They have to be. After all it's us or them. And that becomes clearer and clearer every day. What they say about Martin's novels are that they're crypto-Fascist. I don't think that's quite fair. But I see what they mean. It's that atavistic Liberalism, and will he ever get out of it?

The other day Martin was actually attacking the USSR.

43

Over those trials. And he didn't seem to see at all where it leads to if you attack the USSR. After all, they're the one sixth of the whole world that's leading Socialism everywhere. Everyone else who goes there says how wonderful it is. The workers really in charge of their own lives, controlling the means of production and ensuring that the result is shared out fairly. That's what Socialism means. Not paying huge dividends to the ship-owners and leaving the men to starve. You can't attack the USSR, you really can't! It's the great hope for all of us. As long as it's there and powerful and strong, there's hope for all the workers of the whole world. They can see it's successful and they can see it works, and they can compare it with the chaos that exists under capitalism. There's no unemployment in the USSR, not one single man. There's freedom, too. None of this bourgeois morality that stifles our lives, and the USSR is the one country that really stands up to Hitler, and yet we won't make any alliance with them to stop him!

Yet there was Martin attacking them openly. That doesn't do any good: that's what I call disruptive. And what makes it so much worse is that Martin has this great influence with the young. It's irresponsible of him to undermine their faith in the tremendous advances being made in one sixth of the earth's surface!

'What do the Bookshop crowd think of Martin?'

Well, you know, they're a very diverse lot, all sorts really, young intellectuals, writers, artists and some layabouts too. They're none of them that I've met really seriously interested in politics. Just in a general way. So they all do admire Martin tremendously. If they really knew about politics, they'd see where he's destructive, but as it is they regard him as their kind of spokesman, and whenever the press interviews him and he comes out with some opinion that shocks the bourgeoisie, they're delighted and feel he's spoken up for them. And he's very good at that, I agree. He doesn't mind what he says in public or how 'revolutionary' he is. Only it isn't revolutionary in the pure sense, you understand. He hasn't really studied Marxism, you see, as you find out when you talk to him. He just has a very generous view—because he is very generous-minded—that Capitalism is an unjust system and that it's got to be changed. But he isn't a scientific Socialist, just an emotional one. But I admit it works: he does shock, which is a very good thing to do. And the young love it when he does.

But sooner or later he'll have to see that that isn't enough, that, if things are going to be changed, it can't be done just by shocking people. He'll have to understand the historical process and see that that leads inevitably to the Dictatorship of the Proletariat, and that's the only way a real change can be made.

Author's Note

Harry's view of Martin had, only naturally, undergone a good many changes. When I first knew them at the beginning of their affair, you couldn't make even the mildest criticism of Martin without Harry flying to his defence. He had that kind of loyalty which is absolutely intense and one-tracked for the enthusiasm of the moment. Everything Martin did was wonderful. He was always quoting at me what Martin had said, and he virtually knew Martin's novels by heart.

That was, of course, bound to change. It was too intense to last. But he was still ready to come to Martin's defence if he was seriously attacked. And he wouldn't let Gavin talk about him as he did to me. His real complaint seemed to be that Martin was excluding him more and more from his life:

When I first joined him, Harry said, we used to do everything together. He never went out without taking me along. I used to type all his work for him. I knew I wasn't very good at it, but I think it helped a bit. Then I used to do all the meals and see to the flat and all. Perhaps I did get a little lazy about it, but it was always done sooner or later, wasn't it? And if I forgot about meals, we could always go out, couldn't we?

I think he began to be jealous as I made friends in my own right. Gavin and you and Lady Nellie and all. I believe he really felt that I only ought to know you with him. Underneath, that is. He wanted to own me. I was to be *his* secretary and *his* wife and *his*, altogether. Just what he chose to let me be, or to make me. Well, you can't have that, can you? I mean I must be allowed a life of my own, mustn't I? I don't mean it was sexual jealousy. I don't think it was, I really don't. It was jealousy of me being someone in my own right.

You know how bitchy he is about me linking up with the Party? That's what I mean, you see. Just because he can't make up his mind where he finally stands, he's really furious because I can. And naturally things have been much worse since this, because I'm bound to oppose him politically, aren't I? I mean, we all know where this kind of in-between position lands one in the end, don't we? And he knows as well as anyone really. But he's stubborn.

And then there's sex, too. Although I said he wasn't jealous, and I mean it, all the same he's not liberal about that. He's some kind of puritan actually. He thinks casual sex is all wrong really. I say, what's wrong with it? It does no one any harm, does it? But he says it does. Yet he admits he has a liking for it himself, and can't resist it. But he doesn't approve of it, for himself either. He thinks it's all part of what he calls 'the homosexual dilemma', and he really seems to think it isn't just the same for normals. Well, I mean, how obstinate can you get? The thing is that he wishes he were normal, and even tries to pretend he is sometimes. But I know he's not and never will be. If he was, I wouldn't stand in his way, I really wouldn't. But it's all make-believe with him.

There's a lot of make-believe about Martin. I suppose there's bound to be with a novelist, isn't there? But it isn't easy living with someone when you don't know whether they're being serious or not. You see, sometimes he may be just sort of trying out an attitude to see what it's like, and then when I take it seriously, he laughs at me.

He laughs at me a lot now. He won't take anything I do seriously. That's the worst of all. I know I oughtn't to mind; it's just him being funny in his way. But I do mind. It takes away my dignity. I never go out with him now practically, because sooner or later he's laughing at me. Against me, I mean. I do think he oughtn't to do that, don't you?

Do you know, I sometimes think he's trying to edge me out? But I'm not having that, I can tell him. If he's doing it to make me want to go, he's going the wrong way about it. There are bound to be ups and downs in a relationship, aren't there? And we're just having one of the downs. But we'll get through it, you'll see. This phase will pass and we'll settle down into something steady. We can't throw three years away, can we? Besides, I love him.

Actually I feel sorry for Martin sometimes, I really do. He's got himself into such a tangle over his politics. He can't see things straight any longer. He's really just a Liberal at heart like his father and all of them. But he does see where that sort of thinking lands you, but he can't take the next step. He's come out as a Socialist and really thinks he is one because he's horrified by what he sees going on all round us. But it's no good being just horrified, is it? It's

47

what you do that counts. That's what the CP says, and it's right about that. It's no good thinking the Labour Party are going to do anything about unemployment. Look what happened when they were in! Nothing! And now they're broken. No, if it's going to be done, we've got to do it, we, the workers. And that's where Martin sticks. He doesn't trust the workers, not really.

'Isn't it the Communists he doesn't trust?'

Yes, but he ought to, oughtn't he, after all he's seen? You see, where Martin's Socialism really began was when he went to Berlin after Oxford. He's often told me about those days. It was the rise of Hitlerism. He saw it at first hand. And he admits the Communists were the only ones who really opposed the Nazis flat out. The Social Democrats wavered, as they always do, don't they? And you know it was Martin's description of all this that really set me going. He taught me that the Communists were the ones who really fought. But now he seems to have forgotten that.

'But he's still violently anti-Nazi?'

Oh yes, he is that. Having seen what the Nazi terror really means, he's more against it than almost anyone. Well, you are if you've seen it, aren't you? And he tries his hardest to persuade everyone that Hitler is the great danger of our time and can't understand how the ruling classes don't seem to notice or care. But as I tell him, it's in their class interest not to, isn't it? It all depends on class interest, doesn't it? The ruling class secretly approve of Hitler. He's doing just what they'd really like to do, isn't he? Persecuting the Jews and intellectuals and wiping out Socialism and Communism by force. They really admire him for that, and wish they could do the same. Because, after all, Hitler just represents the last effort of capitalism to maintain itself, doesn't he?

But Martin won't see this; he says once you attribute
48

everything to class interests alone, you are lost. It's because he's a writer, you see, and it's over writing that he sticks out really. Because we say that all bourgeois art and philosophy and thought is only a kind of opium to the people, hiding the reality from them. And he won't have that. The writers he admires, he says, are our ancestors and can't be just wiped off the map and dismissed as class enemies.

'I understand his thinking that as a writer, don't you?'

Yes in a sort of way, but when it comes to politics, it is all a question of class, isn't it? And action has to be judged by whether it's for the workers or against them, doesn't it? And even there he won't agree. He's so stubborn, as I say. And we have terrible arguments about it now. He's very unpopular with the Party actually, but they're realists and see he's important. He has such an influence with the young. So it's my job to try and convert him and that's what I do. But oh he's stubborn!

'You think he still has a great influence with the young?'

Oh yes! You should see him with them. I used to go up to Oxford and Cambridge with him quite regularly. He was a terrific hit there always, he really was. He'd go up to give a talk to one of the Societies they have and the meetings were always full to overflowing; and there'd be terrific competition over who should carry him away afterwards and we'd generally stay there a couple of days and be asked out all the time.

Lunch with one lot, tea in someone's rooms, dining at High Table, and then back to someone else's rooms, and crowds of people sitting all over the floor and packed in everywhere. That's the effect he had. It's extraordinary, really. He had this attraction, that's what it was. Partly physical, partly the way he had of sort of stumbling towards the truth. Never laying down the law. Never seeming superior, but sort of exploring with them the way we had to think now, whether it hurt or not, if you see what I mean.

And he was always ready to admit that he didn't find it easy to know what he did believe and what he didn't, and to see all the contradictions in any position you took up, and was always ready to admit his own inconsistencies and that giggle would come out—and they were charmed. That's what they were, they were charmed into believing what he believed. And behind it was this sincerity which really was genuine. When Gavin says he's faking it all he's quite wrong. Martin really does believe that sooner or later the whole mass of the people have got to take over and work together. It's how it's to be done we quarrel over.

Author's Note

If Gavin wasn't impressed by Martin, that was hardly surprising. For Gavin was one of those intellectuals who are, so to speak, professionally unimpressed by everybody, and who take pleasure in debunking anyone with a reputation. The common capacity of hero-worship had been left entirely out of his make-up. Someone had only to build up a reputation as a writer, a talker, a sexual athlete, or a beauty, for Gavin to set about trying to find the cracks in the surface. It was for some such reason, I think, that he was determined to find Oxford 'a ghastly place'. Everyone, myself included, told him of its enchantments, and how lucky he was to be there and to have the chance to share its wonders and opportunities; so it was up to him to prove them wrong. Oxford, he said, was dowdy and provincial; its famous figures were a lot of phonies, the place itself ruined by the traffic and the industrial development, his fellow undergraduates a set of unsophisticated schoolboys pretending to be grown-up. He was making himself splendidly miserable there.

In this same spirit, he was not standing for any nonsense about Martin being wonderful:

MARTIN'S FILE III

It isn't that I don't like Martin, Gavin said, I do. But he's just too good to be true. I mean all that stuff about the way this society warps us, do you think he really believes it? Well, I suppose he believes it, yes. But then he can afford to, can't he? He's one of those people who would be very happy living in a Socialist state on a private income. Yes, I know I'm bitchy about him! But what the hell! It's time someone was. He gets away with it much too easily.

You should have seen him at Oxford. He was always coming up there and launching that great suffering face into a sea of undergraduates, and you could watch them all swooning to gather round and hold him up. He's so clever with it, too. He isn't like some of the people who came down as ardent believers and preached exciting sermons to the already converted, whipping up their ardour. No, Martin's line was quite different. He hung out his conscience painfully in front of them and after a lot of soul-searching came down on the proper side. Much more effective—in fact, devastating.

What gets me about it, is that that isn't the Martin we know in ordinary life—or rather it is, but in private life, just between us, it's forgivable. More than that, it's natural, natural, that is, to him. But when the same thing is done in public—that sort of parading of an innocent naïvety—then there's something nasty, something exhibitionist about it.

That's it—he's an emotional 'flasher', flashing not his cock but his conscience, to draw attention. 'Isn't this a lovely desirable conscience,' he's saying all the time he's in public. 'No one has such a delicate, tender, subtle conscience as me.' Yet when it's all finished, when every scruple has been weighed in the most accurate of balances, when every *pro* has been measured against every *con*, it all adds up to the same thing. Should one join the Communist Party?—which in the last analysis he doesn't, and won't, do.

Oh yes, I like his novels—quite. But they are rather tarred with the same brush. They're saved, of course, by being funny as well, really wickedly funny, sometimes— that's the effect of the giggle we get in private which punctures the balloon of intensity he's blown up. But that giggle doesn't work so well in public, does it? Not for me, anyhow. It's only the public *persona* I can't do with, you understand. All that blushing and stammering and seeming shy, when he's not shy at all. It's part of the act, and it's growing on him.

He can be maddening in private, too, of course, but that is different. I think he thinks I'm a very bad influence on Harry. You see, all this anxiety to get Harry 'on his own feet' is only an evasion of responsibility really. Harry isn't the kind of person to be on his own feet. He doesn't belong on the ground, anyhow. But up in the air. He wants flying, like a kite, and somebody has to manipulate the string. Martin's just too self-engrossed to do it.

I think Martin's incapable of a relationship, because he's so preoccupied with what he himself is thinking or feeling. What do I, Martin Murray, think about the working class? What do I, Martin Murray, feel about the Liberal dilemma? How can I, Martin Murray, reconcile the demands of Party discipline with my role as a writer?

He hasn't time or energy left over for anyone else. He was busy enough at the start of the affair, providing amusements for Harry. Taking him here and there, introducing him to this famous person and that, whisking him off to Venice, Rome, Paris, whenever Harry looked bored. But now it's very different. Now he's got him, Harry's in the way. Harry's boredom is just an infringement on Martin's complete liberty to devote himself to himself. My sympathies are all with Harry. He feels neglected because he is neglected. Make no mistake, Martin, for all his appearance of hesitation and balance, is an absolutely *ruthless* person. He knows exactly what he wants and he intends to get it, and damn everyone else. All the scruples and arguments and haverings come after the decision. What he's really dickering about is not what he's going to do—he knows that exactly. It's how he's going to justify it to himself and the world. He has a passion for self-justification—that's Martin. And all the self-justifying has to be done in public. He has to put himself right with the world, and he's very clever at it. He takes everyone in, because they think that at the moment when he's expressing his doubts, he really is undecided. That's the fallacy. But he always gets away with it.

Yes, I suppose he does disapprove of me. Not surprisingly. He knows I don't fall for all that. I'm one of the non-worshippers. But he graciously forgives me because he knows I'm in a mess, and can't get out of it. And he can't get me out, either. That makes me interesting. If the great Martin Murray can't solve the problems, they must be very grave, mustn't they? So I'm 'interesting' because temporarily insoluble. But the thing is that if a solution was found for me, then I shouldn't be interesting any more. I should just be dropped.

Author's Note

At this time I had a rather revealing account of Martin in action. He had agreed to address a great Democratic Rally in the St Pancras Town Hall, and was evidently regretting it every moment. 'They aren't meetings in the ordinary democratic sense,' he said. 'They're just stamping grounds for the faithful.'

Martin might have produced another equally cogent reason for regretting his decision, namely that he was an extremely bad speaker on this kind of formal occasion. He was perfectly effective as long as he was just talking to clubs or societies, because with them he did just talk, turning the occasion into a conversation. But his formal speeches were nearly always disastrous. He blushed, stammered and lost his line of thought at the least interruption and generally made a fool of himself. He was quite aware of this, but it didn't deter him from accepting invitations to speak, not, as Gavin used to say, out of vanity, but because he had this rather remarkable capacity for not minding if he did make a fool of himself. His friends might blush for him, but he didn't care. What did it matter, in the long run, if he did? A temporary embarrassment for himself and others wasn't all that important. If it was an occasion on which he ought to speak, he would, and if the price to be paid was his looking a bit of a fool, what did that really matter?

I have obviously taken a novelist's liberty when it came to writing up Martin's description to me of the actual meeting:

MARTIN'S FILE IV

The Town Hall was full, Martin said, when we, the speakers, came out on to the platform. The faithful had come in their thousands. There was a sprinkling of the opposition, I noticed. Some of Mosley's bully boys scattered round the back, and up in front a small group of cheerful young Tories who were just there for the lark. There were less than a dozen of them and their counter-cries weren't making much impression against the slogans chanted by the faithful. As we came on, the meeting rose to its feet and sang the Red Flag, except for this little Tory group who were desperately trying Rule Britannia.

The Platform, except for me, consisted of old regulars: Pollitt, the Communist Party Leader, Pritt, the KC, the Dean of Canterbury, and so on. They said just what the audience had come to hear, and were cheered to the echo. They denounced Hitler, they denounced the Government for not denouncing Hitler. They demanded that active steps should be taken to oppose the Dictators, and they violently opposed allowing our Government of crypto-Fascists to rearm. They proved to their complete satisfaction, and the satisfaction of the audience, that the National Government were a collection of spineless reactionaries who encouraged rearmament for the profits they got out of it and encouraged unemployment to keep the working-class in its place. They denounced the Labour Party as tools of the bourgeoisie, and they called on the working class to make themselves felt, to seize power and unite with the working classes of the world. And they each finished with a rousing cheer for the USSR, extolled the glories of Soviet democracy and called for an instant alliance with Moscow against the Fascist danger.

There were numbers of interruptions during their speeches, and scuffles at the back: a small free-fight developed for a moment and some of the Mosley boys were flung unceremoniously out, two, at least, of them with bleeding noses. The little party of Tory students up in front had contributed their share of heckling, but in a perfectly good-natured way, and the speakers, all practised old hands, had dealt with them easily enough.

Then came my turn to speak. I was introduced fulsomely by the chairman as 'the most important of our younger novelists who has shown by his example that writing is no ivory tower business and that artists and cultural workers stand behind the working masses'.

I hadn't much liked the not unbrutal way in which the interrupters at the back had been treated, and I didn't much like the chairman's introduction either. But there it was and I had to go on. What I was determined not to do was just echo all the Left-wing slogans. It seemed to me that a Rally for Democracy ought to consider some of the really difficult problems that confront democrats. I wanted to question our too uncritical admiration of the USSR and also our policy of rearming. I wanted to make them think. I'd prepared this speech, and though I sensed it was against the spirit of the meeting, I determined to give it.

'Yes, we writers, too, have to face problems as everyone else has, as we know what has happened to most of our fellow writers in Germany and Italy. So we can't afford to sit back and take no part in a struggle that threatens us as much as it threatens anyone. But a writer isn't a politician, he is looking for a very different kind of truth and his first duty is not to any Party slogan, but to the truth, the truth that he discovers in his writing and which makes his writing worth while.

'I've listened carefully to what the other speakers have been saying, and I must in all honesty admit that some of it I find puzzling. I suppose that politically it is right to try and find the basis for an alliance with the USSR. But the other speakers seem to me to gloss over too easily some of the difficulties that arise over this.'

The hall became distinctly uneasy at this, and there were shouts of 'Long Live the USSR!' from some of the supporters. But from the little group of Tories up in front came the question 'What about the Trials?'

[Author's Note: *The Soviets had lately been undergoing one of those clean-ups in which Stalin had liquidated his enemies after public Trials in which there had been many of the open-court 'confessions' which so puzzled everyone but the very faithful.]*

'Yes, what about the Trials?' repeated the other young Tories, and three or four 'stewards' pushed their way menacingly up to the front as if to 'deal with them'.

'No, leave them alone,' I shouted. 'They are quite right to enquire about the Trials. I enquire about the Trials. I want some answer. I'm not satisfied that these Trials have any relation to democracy as we know it, and this is one of the things that disturb me when I hear this so-called Rally for Democracy supporting the USSR so uncritically.'

At this point the Chairman jumped up and assured us that he had been at the Trials in the Soviet Union, that they were as fair and just as any trials anywhere. Indeed fairer and juster. They represented proletarian fairness and justice, and wasn't it well known that this was the fairest fairness and the justest justice in the world?

He sat down to howls of applause, and I realised I should get nowhere. But I knew what I wanted to say and I was going to say it.

'If the Chairman really believes that, he would believe anything,' I went on. ('Hear, hear!' from the young Tories, 'Shame!' from all over the hall.) 'And this is just one of the things that worries me in all these questions. Aren't we all encouraging ourselves to believe just what we want to believe and not trying really to face the issues? Take disarmament. Is it really true that we ought to shout *for* disarmament and yet oppose rearmament when Germany is rearming as fast as we all know she is? Aren't we simply following old shibboleths when we say that the call to rearm is a call only for more private profits for the arms manufacturer.' (Shouts of 'Isn't it?', 'What about Krupps?', 'Butter not guns', 'Hear, hear!' from the young Tories.)

57

'Who is going to oppose Fascism if we haven't the arms to do it with?' ('The working class!', 'Hear, hear!' from the Tories.)

And at this point six tough young stewards who had moved up earlier pounced on the young Tories, and began flailing with their fists. Two were wearing knuckle-dusters, I saw them. The young men were bashed about, teeth came out, noses bled. There was complete uproar in the hall. Shouts of 'Chuck 'em out', 'Let 'em have it', etc. I turned round and protested violently to the Chairman to try and make him intervene. It was a short sharp brutal struggle, and the young Tories were bundled or carried out to the cheers of most of the hall.

It was just the sort of exhibition you see if you go to a Mosleyite meeting and the last thing I'd expect at a Rally for Democracy. When it was over and order was restored, I managed to say as loudly as I could, 'And if you think that's a good example of Rallying for Democracy, I have nothing more to say at all.' And I sat down.

There was a distinctly uneasy pause, I'm delighted to say, before the Chairman stepped forward and produced once again the revivalist clichés to get the meeting going again. Out they all came, the same old slogans. The struggle against Fascism. Working-class unity. The unemployed. The crypto-Fascist Government. Alliance with the USSR. And with another rousing singing of the Red Flag the meeting came to an end, and people began filing out.

On the platform several people began arguing bitterly with me.

'Don't you see, Comrade,' a fierce little CP member was saying, 'what happens when you don't support the Party line? You end by being applauded by the very enemies of the working class!'

'Don't you think,' I insisted, 'that it's right to put to ourselves the other side?'

'There's plenty to put the other side,' said the fierce little man. 'They're doing it all over England. You needn't do it for them. There's only one test. Who were the people who supported you? Tories and Fascists! You must be wrong.'

'But wasn't what I was saying the truth?'

'A very dangerous thing, the truth,' said the fierce little man. 'The truth is what we believe.'

'And there's no such thing as objective truth?'

'Certainly not,' I was roundly told. 'All truth is class truth. The Tory class applauded you because what you said was Tory truth. The workers shouted you down, because they know what's their truth.'

'I think your speech was unfortunate, Murray.' The Chairman came over to join the discussion. 'Whatever you may think privately about the Soviet Trials, for instance, surely it's better to keep it to oneself?'

'But why?' I asked. 'Do you think they were anything but faked?'

'Whatever I thought personally,' the Chairman said judiciously, 'I wouldn't muddle an audience like this by saying so. What good does that do?'

'The truth always does good,' I asserted.

'We don't know the truth,' said the Chairman, 'not absolutely. So isn't it better to keep off the subject?'

'Do you support the USSR whatever it does?' I asked him.

'I know that the USSR is for the working masses of the world,' said the Chairman unctuously, 'and knowing that, I'm bound to support them, yes.'

What can one say to that? 'As a writer I can't subscribe to that sort of blanket approval.'

'Perhaps you'll realise, then, why we don't trust writers.' The Chairman smiled as if he were hoping this remark would smooth things over. But it started me up again.

'I suppose you mean you're afraid we might tell the truth about what really happened at this Rally for Democracy?'

'How do you mean "what really happened"?' asked the Chairman.

'I mean,' I said furiously, 'that your thugs behaved just as badly as Mosley's thugs. Which shows what you really think of free speech!'

'Did you want your speech interrupted, Comrade Murray?'

'They were doing no harm. It was an open meeting. They had a right to be there and to express their opinions if they did it reasonably, and they did.'

'Do you grant the right of free speech to the Fascists, too?'

'They weren't Fascists; they were just young Conservative students.'

'That doesn't answer my question. Do you grant the right of free speech to Fascists, to attack the Jews and the working classes?'

That, of course, was rather a difficult one. 'I can't just answer yes or no to that. It's more complicated.'

'Not for me,' said the Chairman. 'I don't, and I ordered those boys to be thrown out if you want to know.'

'And do you condone the violence with which it was done?'

'There's worse things ahead for all of us than a few missing teeth and a broken nose, and you had better get used to the fact,' said the Chairman and went off.

I don't know what to say about it, Martin summed it up. Of course, my speech, such as there was of it, was silly. I oughtn't to have plunged in like that. I ought to have worked round to it gradually. I'm a hopeless speaker. It just got my goat, all those pious platitudes the Platform handed out, and the silly audience applauding without thinking. Yet they aren't silly entirely; they're much less silly than a corresponding Tory audience would be. They're fighting more on the right side, in so far as there is a right side. Yes, in fact, I still think we . . . they; anyhow . . . are more right than the Tories are. But right or wrong—what on earth do the terms mean in this hopeless position we're all in? That fierce little man—he's the chief Party spokesman —saying never, never, never would he vote to give this Government arms . . . but what other Government have we got? That's the illusion they live under, that, by rallying for democracy, they make themselves powerful. They feel powerful in the mass like that, and this seems to blind them to the fact that they represent nothing but a handful of the fervent. I don't know, I think I'll go abroad again. To Vienna. At least what goes on there isn't just make-believe.

[Author's Note: *And, in fact, he left with Harry for Vienna the next week.*]

III

HARRY WATSON

Author's Note

I was seeing a good deal of Martin at this time and politics weren't his only preoccupation. He was also very bothered by the problem of Harry. When Harry suspected that Martin was trying to edge him out, Harry was quite right. That's just what Martin was trying to do. He had come to the conclusion that their relationship was now a barren one, that they had each given and received as much as could be given and received from each other and that it was time they parted. Of course, as I reminded him, it was easier for him to accept this than it was for Harry. Yet though I was very fond of Harry and saw his point of view, I sympathised with Martin too.

It wasn't only that Martin at this time was making his experiments in heterosexuality. It was also that Harry had virtually ceased to perform any function in Martin's life. If he had begun off as a sort of secretary-wife, he had by now ceased to be either. They had got in a woman to do such charring as was done, and in fact their flat looked increasingly scruffy. Harry had given up cooking and they took their meals out. Harry was never up in the mornings in time to get Martin's breakfast for him and, in the bohemian manner of the day, Martin rummaged round for himself. Harry had never made a success of the typing, and that went out to an agency.

Martin was not, perhaps unfortunately, the sort of person to complain about these things as such. But they were symptoms of what he came to regard as a deeper malaise, as the first entry in Harry's file shows:

62

The trouble about the Harrys of this world, Martin would say, is quite simply that their tastes have outrun their abilities. Call it my fault, if you like. But if it hadn't been me, it would have been someone else, and, after all, there were plenty before me. I suppose in a decently organised society the problem wouldn't arise. Why shouldn't a Guardsman like Harry have tastes for the kind of expensive luxuries we all have a taste for? And if he has, why shouldn't he be able to gratify them as much as anyone else? But society being what it is, there isn't really any way of his doing it except by hanging on to someone who can afford to pay for them. Then the moment he does that, he begins to feel guilty and to take it out—such is human nature—on that one person.

Guilt causes half the trouble in our society. Harry feels guilty at being dependent on me. I feel guilty at having made him dependent on me. He feels guilty when he's extravagant. I feel guilty at not giving him enough. He feels guilty about being so lazy. I feel guilty about trying to push him into doing something that nothing would persuade *me* to do.

'Isn't he busy and happy working for the Party, now?'

Do you really think so? Do you really think that all that pious puritanism of theirs is really Harry's cup of tea? I don't. I can't really make out his reason for working with them. It really isn't his sort of line by nature. I think it's simply another way of trying to make me feel guilty. No, I do really. He knows what I think of them. He knows there's a constant pressure on me to make a public declaration allying myself with them, and he knows I don't intend to be caught like that. He thinks by linking up with them himself, he's somehow putting me in the wrong.

'Has everything he does got to be related to you?'

Of course! Why pretend? And it isn't just vanity on my part. It's the nature of relationships, especially this kind of relationship. Harry's really intensely feminine—which is why I distrust this Party nonsense. He's really a wife. But a wife without a wife's status. And this leaves him out on a limb. When I say he's intensely feminine, I mean that he has no other real interests except the domestic ones, and relationships. That's all he has to occupy himself with. He wouldn't, by the way, be a good wife, as some boys would be, because he's lazy and dirty, really, and sloppy. Natural reaction against the Guards' discipline, I suppose.

The trouble about our sorts of relationship is that they are almost in the conventional pattern, but never quite. They're always just out of kilter. I suppose if I could only fully accept the relationship as a marriage, I might be able to make it work better. I could insist on his doing all the housework and the cooking instead of getting someone else in to do it, thus robbing him of his *raison d'être*. But I should have to badger and badger to get it done.

No, wait a minute. I'm not being quite honest there. The fact is I don't regard him as a wife, and can't. It would seem to me demeaning to his manhood to turn him into one. I don't want him feminine. I want him masculine. I'm not quite sure why. But I think underneath I may really resent that femininity of his—and yet without it how can the relationship be expected to work? The answer is, of course, that it doesn't. Yet it's not as easy as that. Because, also, in a kind of way, it does. And whenever we come to the point where we talk of parting, we can neither of us face it. So, the relationship may not 'work', yet obviously we each mean so much to the other that it can't just be snapped. Is there any way out? I don't see one.

I wonder if there's always some flaw in the homosexual relation, inevitable and incurable? Isn't it by its nature a substitute relationship in which each of the two expects the

64

other one to be something other than they are, because each of them is a substitute for something else? Acceptance is fundamental to any relationship, and it seems as if just what we cannot any of us do is accept the other person for what they are. We inevitably muddle them with the ideal father or mother or son or brother or whatever it is we are looking for, and then blame them for not coming up to that ideal.

Poor Harry! I've proved a most inadequate father. Yet I'm not going to blame myself too much. When I first met him, Harry had all the qualities that everyone admires in him. But they hadn't all been able to flower. And I certainly haven't taken them away. What I've added in the way of chances to develop, he hasn't entirely been able to make use of. That isn't my fault. But he deserved to have those chances. It was up to him what he made of them. If that sounds hard, well, one has to be hard at a certain point. If two non-swimmers are caught in a current, it's no use their both drowning if one can get away, whatever it costs that one in guilt to abandon the other.

But when all's said and done, he's the most affectionate and warm-hearted of creatures, and that's rare enough for one to be grateful for; and when I look round and see how some people's boy-friends behave, I know I've every reason to be grateful. But, alas, counting our blessings is all very well, but they never quite add up to what one wants and is wilfully determined to have.

Author's Note

This struggle between Martin and Harry occupied a good deal of all our attention as we watched it developing; and it was, indeed, of more importance than we realised at the time, since its outcome was to lead to their going to Spain and what followed from that. Gavin, only naturally, was a violent partisan for Harry, and not only because he was 'anti-Martin'. It was also because he was at one time almost certainly in love with Harry, though I see he was rather inclined to discount the extent of it when I asked him whether he had been:

HARRY'S FILE II

Yes, I suppose I was in a sort of way, Gavin said. But I'm not sure it wasn't really all in the head, if you know what I mean. I mean, yes, we did go to bed together, and it was fun. But my 'being in love' was really just perhaps because I thought it was time I was. Not entirely. But quite a lot. You know how it is with all those songs we have. They're so good one finds oneself imitating their sentiments. I think Cole Porter is the greatest influence on our age, and partly because he's so astute at drawing us in. 'Every time we say good-bye, I die a little.' Well, that echo of the poem is frightfully good, and adds just the fatal drop to the narcotic that takes one under. And one surrenders.

And, yes, there is something impelling and terrible about the telephone sitting there, and one waiting desperately for it to ring and be the right person; and the hours one spends imagining what the other person is doing, who he's with and why he's not with you. Does it mean he doesn't want to be or he can't be? Or standing outside cinemas when you've arranged to meet, and them not coming. They're always late. Why are they always late? And, then, their wretched incapacity, incapacity, I mean, to match the intensity of one's own feelings. Harry hasn't any real feelings, I some-times think. He certainly hadn't for me. I amused him some-times. But you'd never feel Harry was 'Past the plunge of plummet'.

66

If

> One the long night through must lie
> Spent in star-defeating sighs

it wasn't Harry, you may be sure.

Yet all the same he had a feeling for those things, too. He has, curiously, a real feeling for poetry, you know. He loved the Housmans when I read them to him and learns reams of Auden off by heart. So it isn't that it isn't there, but just that it wasn't there for me. And I don't think it really is for anyone, not even Martin.

Are those songs we all hum now, sad, masochistic, all with an ache in them, and those particular poems, too, just all auto-erotic? Is it ourselves we're just thinking about in isolation all the time? I dare say.

Who is it we're parted from, then? Who is it who never comes, who never rings, who is never there when we want him, and who, when he is there, never comes up to our expectations? Well, in my case I made it Harry.

Harry's a very deceptive personality, you see. First there's this warmth of feeling. Everyone notices that at first. It's something he gives off like a civet cat its smell. And you can easily deceive yourself into thinking that it's specially for you. But it isn't. It's just a sort of generalised odour, pleasant and enveloping, but it's as much for everyone as it is for you.

Then there's the gaiety. That was, as it seemed, perpetual, at least until he began flirting with the Party. It was something wholly spontaneous, and there from the first moment you met. A quality of delight in being, that I found very enviable. It would suddenly break out into a dance. In a room he was always half dancing, just swinging, swaying with sheer pleasure at life. That's been educated out of all of us. It was Harry's precious legacy from the collier's cottage.

An awful lot of nonsense is talked about the proletarian

virtues. They're supposed to have a spontaneous vitality that we've lost and a lot of balls like that. But with Harry, it wasn't balls, as I can assure you it was with the lumpy, sour-faced boys and girls he introduced to me from his 'Cell'. They were just a lot of self-conscious young prigs.

But Harry really had it, he really did, and that was what was so sad about his mixing himself up with the Party. You could see it going, almost visibly, as he tried to match their puritan seriousness.

Harry isn't a serious person, never was and never could be. Trying to be so is like wearing the wrong kind of clothes, all starchy and formal when his whole point was to be relaxed and casual. These days, there seem to be so few people about that are like that. Spencer—my brother—used to call us frivolous. But I was never frivolous, more's the pity. Harry really had the purest kind of frivolity, and it was so fresh and so refreshing. He bubbled wherever he went.

Unfortunately Martin wasn't capable of appreciating that quality, or rather, having appreciated it—presumably it was what attracted in the first place—he couldn't let it rest at that. He was always trying to 'improve' Harry. And I blame him for Harry's ridiculous 'conversion'. Harry didn't need improving, all he needed was space, time and absence of pressure, to let him be what he was. Try to improve him and you inevitably ruin him.

I think Harry was the most guilt-free person I'd ever met. If there's one thing our class education does breed, it's guilt. Look at us, Martin, me, all of us, riddled with guilt. Harry seemed to be totally without it, and this gave his enjoyment of everything—sex, a good dinner, getting drunk, a gay evening—a special quality of sparkle which none of us could manage.

Perhaps he ought to have stayed a tart really. He had all the qualities of a really high-class tart or male courtesan. First this lack of guilt, then a high power of appreciation of anything done for him, and a pure belief in the absolute value of pleasure. He should never have been attached, never have been tied. That's fatal to his kind of immediacy of response. It was why a love affair with him was doomed from the outset, and I kind of knew that, but couldn't help myself; and perhaps it only became completely clear as the affair ground to a halt.

The moment he was attached to Martin, I now think, he was doomed. Nothing ought ever to be expected of such characters, nothing ever demanded, especially not such guilt-making things as loyalty or response-in-kind. They ought to be completely free to come or go, to be late or on time, to like or merely to accept. But not to love, that's asking the one thing they can't give; not to be loyal, that's the one thing they can't be; not to match up to different standards, they are bound to fall below them.

Well, now, Harry's a gonner. That's what I really think if you ask me. All this Party stuff is sheer against the grain. It'll simply bring out all the worst in him, all the envy and hate. His inner nature will be warped, his passion for freedom frustrated, and goodness knows where he'll end up. In goal, I expect.

Oh, we shall often have glimpses and patches of the old Harry. We shall still be able to catch some gleams of life from him. But I expect they'll get rarer and rarer. It's very sad.

HARRY'S FILE III

[Nellie had nothing but the greatest admiration for Harry.]
He's a wonderful example, she told me, of just the kind of drive and vitality which Socialism could release in the whole of the people, if we gave it the chance. Isn't it extra-

ordinary to think of him with that background turning out so well? Brought up in a collier's cottage and then conscripted into the Guards? In ordinary circumstances no one would ever have known what a tremendous potentiality there was there. And to think that there are hundreds of thousands—no, millions—of boys like him who will never have his chance under our present system!

That's the terribly wasteful thing about it, as I keep telling David—you know, that awful brother of mine. The system never allows their potentialities to blossom. We've got to change it. And that's another thing you can't help admiring about Harry. Some boys, introduced suddenly to everything exciting, as he has been, would have been content to just grab it and enjoy it for themselves. But Harry's really come to see that if he can make as much of life as he can, so could the thousands he has left behind. And he's doing something about it.

Not like Gavin, who does absolutely nothing except upset his poor mother. Of course, Harry's been lucky in coming under the influence of someone like Martin. I suppose that, there, he could hardly have helped realising that there was something wrong with things and that it *could* be put right. Because it could, you know; Harry isn't the only one. Have you noticed that there's something quite different about the working classes? They aren't—I don't know what it is—inhibited? . . . like our boys. Take my Pugh. There's a tremendous potential there, I'm sure of it. But that ghastly school, instead of realising it, twists it in some way. And then in the holidays there's nothing to go back to except his reactionary step-father and the whole Tory background. So, all that vitality—and there's any amount of vitality there—goes to waste.

'To get back to Harry . . .'

Yes, Harry. Well, no one need worry about Harry. Martin does, I know. But then I don't think Martin is a fair judge in this case. He's too close to him. And do you know what I think? I think Martin is just a little bit jealous of Harry's new activities. He used to complain that Harry did nothing and squandered his days. Yet now that Harry's busying himself with all this political activity, Martin only laughs at him. He won't take it seriously, which is very bad for Harry. Harry needs the encouragement. And after all it was Martin who got him interested, so it's up to Martin to encourage the interest he's aroused, isn't it?

Altogether, I can't help feeling that Martin's not playing quite fair by Harry. You can't take someone up like that and then just drop them, can you? What he tells Harry is that he must try and make himself independent, and he's sure, he's quite sure, he's able to do it. Well, so am I! Everybody likes Harry. He has so many friends, and he fits in so well. He's quite capable of standing on his own feet now. But, of course, it isn't possible with all this unemployment. That's another crime this system is guilty of: and there's that rich, stupid old mother of mine sitting in the Boltons saying that the men don't want to work. How dare she!

Well, Harry's an example. He's always saying to me that he would get a job if only he could. You just can't find them. Martin ought to understand that, if anyone does. But he goes on nagging and nagging. Harry comes round here in a real state sometimes after those perpetual rows with Martin. As if it was his fault! As if there weren't two or three million men in the same boat!

'And you think Harry really wants to get a job?'

I'm sure of it. He talks about it a lot. In fact I was even prepared to see if my brother David couldn't fit him in somewhere. But Harry wouldn't let me. He said he wasn't going to be responsible for me humiliating myself by asking. He's so thoughtful in that kind of way! All the same I did tackle David about it, and he was prepared to find something

71

for Harry. But Harry said he wasn't going to be pushed in by the back door. He couldn't approve of the nepotism that goes on—and, of course, he's quite right. They're always prepared to help each other—people like David. So they get whatever jobs are going. It isn't fair. Harry said he simply wouldn't accept anything on those terms. He'd feel he was supplanting someone who deserved it on merit, and perhaps had a wife and children and everything. I must say I respect him for that, don't you? But it's no good Martin saying he doesn't want a job. Because he does.

I think Harry's the best possible advertisement for Socialism. He's the working-class boy who really has made good, but who hasn't been corrupted by it. I mean he hasn't, like most of them do, joined the class he's climbed into. That's where the ruling class is so subtle. They skim off the cream of the working class and then turn them into ruling-class toadies. That's what David would have liked to do to Harry. He'd have given him a job if I had pressed it. But he'd have expected Harry to be so grateful that he'd have given up his Socialism. I expect that was another reason why Harry wouldn't take a job from David. Because he's not going to be corrupted by that kind of bribe.

There is something incorruptible about Harry. That's what I admire about him. He sticks to his principles through thick and thin. Martin may laugh at him. But Harry isn't put off, and Martin oughtn't to laugh. He ought to realise that he's had all the advantages that Harry has never had. Harry's very serious about his Communism, you see. And he's in a better position than any of us to know the cruelty of the present system. His father suffered all those terrible strikes of the Twenties, and has now been unemployed for five years. Think what that means. Sitting on their hunkers —Harry often describes it to me—day after day except for the parade to the Labour, day after day in those drab little towns with no prospects and no hope. And the dole itself a miserable pittance! Harry's seen it at first hand. He knows what it's like better than any of us.

Author's Note

One of the heroes of the hour at this time was Gavin's brother, Spencer. He had run away from school at a mere fifteen and was lodging in an attic above the Pleaides Bookshop. From there he was editing an anti-Public School magazine and it was from him that Harry had imbibed his first intoxicating sips of orthodox Marxism. Harry had greatly admired him when he first appeared on the scene, and there was something heroic about this boy. He hadn't run away from school to avoid its discipline or because he was being bullied, or just didn't like it—or for any other of the conventional reasons for such escapades.

His wasn't an escapade. It was an intransigent decision, taken by an iron will which had arrived at the inescapable conclusion that a Public School had nothing whatever to offer him. To have reached this decision with such absolute conviction at fifteen argues a mind of uncommon toughness.

When Spencer first arrived in London, Martin was one of the people he contacted and so met Harry. He had his plan already formed for producing a magazine designed to appeal to the intelligentsia in the Public Schools, the growing pacifist minority and the Left-wing generally. Spencer would get it written and edited, and then a devoted band of the faithful would drive round various schools distributing it. Spencer had no illusions about this, as he had none about anything. They would be met with violence from the toughs at any school they penetrated, nor could they expect the magazine to pay.

Martin gave him a cheque, I believe, to start him off, and Harry enlisted himself as a helper. Working side by side

73

with Spencer in this project he learned to admire not only the boy's beaver-like concentration on the job in hand but, too, the frozen discipline which seemed to derive from Spencer's Marxism. Where this child of fifteen had acquired his grasp of this philosophy is a curious question. He must have been born with it inside his head, so fixed and solid it already was.

Harry, as he used to tell me, was both attracted and frightened by Spencer's concentration. For his part he was always ready to break off for coffee in the café opposite, and would cheerfully spend a whole morning gossiping with the various droppers-in, who used the Bookshop as a club. Spencer harried him, and he would buckle to for an hour or so before he found some fresh distraction; but he did pick up from Spencer all the new political catch phrases, and in his own scatter-brained way had begun from that time on to think of himself as a Communist.

Also it was his idea—for which he earned Spencer's praise —that the first school they should try to infiltrate should be the school Pugh Griffiths was at; and he was promptly despatched round to Nellie's to get her to make the necessary contacts. She demurred at first he told me—it might all get into the papers, she said. But when Harry ragged her about this 'upper-class attitude', she laughed and gave in, and through her contact was made. And when they arrived they were expected. The account of this expedition which I duly wrote up and filed was given me by Harry very shortly after:

HARRY'S FILE IV

Pugh had been very efficient, Harry said. He had promised to drum up a reception committee of sympathisers, and had told us that the best time to come was Sunday morning, arriving just after Chapel. That was the time when it was the custom for parents to arrive to take their boys out to lunch, so that our arrival wouldn't be particularly noticeable. We were not to go to the main gate, though, where the cars of the parents parked, but to a side gate further along the drive.

All this went according to plan. There was the main gate, and the visitors' cars drawn up, and the parents standing about waiting. We had timed it right so that there was only five minutes to wait, and then out came Pugh with his four supporters. Everyone was excited at the plan going off so well. The few intellectuals from the school were very thrilled at meeting Spencer, who was a sort of hero to them. They were just like prisoners who were serving a long sentence and wanted to hear all the news from the great outside world; and too much time was spent on all this when we ought to have been smuggling the magazines into the school.

By the time we had got round to that, we had evidently been spotted. Gavin, Pugh, and his supporters eventually took out bundles of copies and went off into the school with them. And then a master approached the van in the drive and asked Spencer what we were doing. Spencer was at the back of van, getting some more bundles ready, even though there were already more in with Pugh and Gavin than any one school could want. But Spencer wasn't practical about this. It was the moral effect of getting as many as possible into this, the first stronghold we had attacked, that counted with him.

When the master approached, Spencer hastily shut up the van, and when he was asked what he was doing, said that he was just visiting.

'Visiting who?' the master wanted to know.

'A cousin,' Spencer said airily.

'Name and House, please,' said the Master.

75

And then Spencer became truculent. 'What's that got to do with you?'

'Everything,' said the master. 'Name and House, please.'

Spencer wasn't going to give Pugh's name of course, and he argued afterwards that what he intended was to stall off the master till Gavin got back. But it would have been better, we all agreed later, if he had been more polite; although we also all thought in the debate afterwards over tactics, that this master must already have got word to his prefects, and stalling was just what, unfortunately, he wanted, too. And, if Spencer had been cleverer, he might have realised this, for it was always part of the get-away plan that if me, Spencer and the van had to make a rapid exit, Gavin would make his own way down to the main road, where there was a pre-arranged rendezvous.

However, Spencer, feeling quite exempt from any school discipline and superior to it, began laying down the law in his most argumentative manner.

'Do you mean to tell me,' he said to the master, 'that I can't come down to visit a cousin of mine without your permission?'

The master smiled, 'You can do whatever you like since you aren't a pupil. But no boy from here can go out without permission.'

'It sounds very antiquated to me,' Spencer said loftily.

'It may be antiquated, but we don't pride ourselves on being advanced here,' the master smiled at him.

'Evidently not,' says Spencer, 'but presumably my cousin who is a pupil here knows your ridiculous rules?'

'He would be wise to, if he wants to save his skin,' said the master.

'Then, in that case, he'll have got permission already, won't he?'

'Yes,' said the master, 'if you *have* a cousin, and he is a member of the school.'

76

'You don't believe it?' Spencer said very fiercely.

'Tell me his name and House, and I might,' said the master.

'I refuse to submit to your bullying. I don't have to,' Spencer said in his most lordly manner.

'You might be wiser to submit to mine,' said the master grinning and giving the first hint of the coming disaster. 'Do you mind opening the back of this van?'

'Yes, I mind very much,' said Spencer.

'I shall have to insist,' said the master.

'By what right?' asks Spencer.

'You are on school property,' said the master, 'and I have every right.'

'I absolutely refuse,' said Spencer.

But it was too late. The time the master had been playing for was up, and six burly boys, rugger forwards, Pugh told us afterwards, came out, and two of them seized Spencer. The others opened the van and shouted:

'Yes, here they are.'

'Perhaps it would be better if you left us, sir,' one of them said to the master. 'We'll deal with it in our own way.'

'Perhaps that would be best,' said the master, grinning.

And they did. First of all they turned Spencer up over one of the mudguards and, using a cane they'd brought with them, they wallopped him as hard as they could and for a very long time. I'd never seen anything like it. It was much worse than any school caning. Spencer was pretty tough, but they went on until he was crying out. Then three of them bundled him off in the direction of the school lake, while the other three began rocking the van as if they'd overturn it.

I wasn't going to get beaten like that, if I could help it, I can tell you. I just sat tight in the driver's seat and said it was nothing to do with me. I was just the driver of this hired van, I told them. I didn't know what the fuss was about. I'd just hired them the van. And then they began rocking it to turn it over, and I said I'd have the law on them, and it would come pretty expensive for them if they did any damage.

Luckily they believed me. And I waited. Then they all came back again and gathered up the rest of the magazines and waited for Spencer to appear dripping from the lake. They'd thrown him in with all his clothes on and it wasn't easy in his condition to carry it off with any dignity. Him dripping and them jeering and tearing up the magazines that were left, in front of him. He took no notice but got in beside me and we shot off.

We found Gavin at the rendezvous. I did think perhaps that Spencer wouldn't think much of me not doing anything to help him when he was set on. But Spencer was a real Marxist about it. He told me I'd done quite right. What could I have done? I'd only have got a lashing too. As it was I didn't. No false heroics, he said. But I can tell you I was shit-scared.

Anyhow fifty magazines, Spencer crowed, had been infiltrated into the enemy encampment. And we gave the story to the *Mail* and they made a headline of it. 'Red Raid on Public School', and it caused quite a stir. But you won't catch me doing it again all the same. I'm not risking getting what Spencer got. You know, he was bleeding afterwards, he really was. It's terrible what they do in those schools, isn't it? Apparently Pugh gets it all the time and his father says nothing. We'd have the law on them if they did anything like that to us. But these upper-class boys just take it. I don't understand it. Not that Spencer could help it in the circumstances, I suppose, though I'm not so sure. He just accepted it, too, as part of the risk. But not for me, thank you.

IV

GAVIN BLAIR SUMMERS

Author's Note

Gavin's file originally consisted largely of extracts from his novel since he was, as we have noticed, the acutest critic of himself and his own predicament. I have included one or two of them, and where I have, I have changed the fake names he invented back to the originals to make it easier for the reader. But I also pursued my own method and got interviews from the others, starting with Harry. I evidently opened by asking Harry if he had ever been in love with Gavin:

GAVIN'S FILE I

No, not really I wasn't, Harry admitted. I was attracted by him, of course. He's so sweet, isn't he? And can be so funny. I knew he was in love with me and I played along for a bit. But I couldn't keep it up. He's very demanding, you see. We'd arrange to meet, and if I was five minutes late there'd be an awful row. And then he wanted to spend every minute of every day together. Well, I couldn't, could I?

Then, he's rather destructive, you know. He did his very best to stop me joining the Party. It meant a lot to me, and he used to attack it from every angle all day and every day. I think he was jealous of it, really. He's a terribly jealous character, Gavin. He can't bear to see anyone having anything he hasn't got, whether it's a girl, a boy or a

79

belief. It was really over the CP we quarrelled. I wasn't going to have my faith in it undermined. Besides, I do believe it would have done him the world of good if he could have joined, too. He needs something to believe in.

'He never seems to know quite what he wants to do. What did you do, before you quarrelled?'

Oh, the usual things, and we still do. We didn't quarrel really, you know. We went to the flicks quite a lot, and he's always great fun to go with. He goes on building up the story after you come out, playing about with it, having fun with it, usually making it all seem absurd, but funny absurd, you know. And we'd go to the Bookshop a good deal and have a good gossip there. There was always someone new or amusing dropping in, and we'd have a chat and a laugh. Spencer, his brother, disapproved of us because he said we were frivolous, and I suppose we were really, but you can't be serious all the time, can you?

What Gavin really liked best was parading Coventry Street and Piccadilly in the evening. After ten, perhaps, and before we went to the Café Royal for supper. It wasn't that he was after any of the boys, but they fascinated him. He liked to stroll along watching them trolling and seeing a pick-up, and speculating what happened after. That was a favourite thing of his. But he didn't like anything grand. I used to love being taken to the Café de Paris, up in the balcony and seeing everybody. But he couldn't stand that. 'What do you want to see them for?' he'd say. But I'd say it was fun, seeing Noël Coward dining with Gertie Lawrence or Diana Cooper or someone. I loved it. But he just snorted at the idea. He was blasé, I suppose. He could see grand people when he went down to his uncle's and all.

But I think I know why he didn't like me joining the Party, really. I wasn't supposed to be serious like that. We each had our roles and were supposed to play them.

I was the innocent, like. I don't mean sex or anything, but in life, if you see what I mean. I was supposed to be the one who just took life as it came, lived in the moment, and enjoyed whatever happened. 'You can't get serious, Harry,' he used to say really crossly. 'You just can't. It's all wrong. It doesn't fit. It'll be the ruin of you.'

What do you think I thought being cast as the perpetual hayseed? I didn't like it. But that was what he wanted of me, and when I wouldn't fit in he got really annoyed. I remember the day I joined the Party; we met in the evening. I felt really excited having come to the decision and made it. Gavin was simply furious. 'You're a bloody fool, Harry,' he said, 'and you're now going to be a bloody bore as well. It's too much. You must be off your head. It was bad enough while you were thinking of it, going through all those ghastly silly arguments which have nothing to do with you. But now you'll start having DOUBTS and going to SERVICES in your CELL every other day and renewing your faith by worship in CONGREGATION—oh, all those dreary demos and marches we'll be condemned to from now on! And you'll carry a banner, I suppose, like the Salvation Army, and march with your chin up singing those dreary German songs. You're going to be intolerable, that's what you're going to be, reading that grubby *Daily Worker* and believing every lie they tell you. And deciding I'm irredeemably frivolous because irredeemably upper-class. And you, the simple collier's son, child of toil and slavery, representative of the new vital masses. It's insupportable. I shan't see you any more.'

'But he did?'

Oh, yes, he did and does. But he never stops going on about it, and now he's the one who's getting boring. Still, I'm very fond of him really. You can't help being, can you? And whenever I wanted a relief from the intensity of the Comrades—and they are a bit intense, you know—

I always turned to Gavin. He was always ready for any distraction there was going. He didn't really know what to do with himself half the time. So if you suggested something, a dinner or a flick or a walk in the park, he was always ready to drop what he was doing, if he was doing anything, and come with you. Mostly he wasn't doing very much.

He had this holiday work they're supposed to do, but he couldn't get down to it. I used to lecture him about it. Because lots of boys would give their eyes to have the chances he has at Oxford and all that, and it's such a waste his doing nothing with it. Besides, it's his duty, isn't it, to make the most of his advantages? But it wasn't any use talking to him like that. 'You're being a bloody bore again, I hate you in your puritan mood.' But I say, it only shows that it's all wrong for people like that to have the advantages when those who could use them don't get the chance.

Then there's this novel he's writing. He's shown us some of it, and me and Martin think it awfully good. But he won't put his back into it and gets discouraged. It's all about himself and his mother, and I come into it. But there, too, because he doesn't believe in anything, he isn't getting anywhere. If he could be less destructive and more positive, I'm sure it would go better. You've got to believe in something, haven't you, or where are you?

GAVIN'S FILE II

[Nellie evidently hadn't much to say for Gavin.]
Of course I've known them for ever—the Blair Summers, Nellie told me. Gavin was a sweet little boy and poor Fanny was so proud of him. It was a terrible shock to her when Spencer—that's Gavin's brother—ran away from school,

and it all got into the newspapers. They're very conventional people really—or certainly he is—the Admiral. Fanny less so. She's an extravagant sort of woman, extravagant with her feelings, I mean. That always made her more fun. She was ashamed really on his behalf—the Admiral's. But she never minded so much about Spencer. I knew him only as a dour, rather scowling boy. I always hoped that they were going to be nice friends for Pugh—my nephew Pugh, you know. I adore Pugh, and he's rather friendless. That's because he doesn't get on with his step-father which I can easily understand. But somehow the boys never hit it off. Spencer was too serious for Pugh, and Gavin was too clever. Pugh isn't clever at all. But it was just as well they didn't. Make friends, I mean. I think Gavin would have been a bad influence.

'Why do you think that? What's wrong with him?'

I don't say there's anything wrong with him exactly. It's just that, well, he pulls everything down. What Pugh really needed—and still needs—is someone to give him a belief in something. You see, I think that he's very promising, hating the life they live in Monmouth and all that. If someone could only give him a lead, he might turn out very well.

'And Gavin can't—or won't?' I said, prompting her back to the subject in hand.

Gavin both won't and can't. You see, he himself is rather disappointing. Fanny's very worried over him. He got this scholarship to Oxford which shows he's clever enough. But he's not doing any good there, Fanny's been told. He doesn't seem to get anything out of life. Of course, it is partly Fanny's fault. She spoiled him terribly. Anything he wanted when he was a boy he could have; and she's so much stronger a character than her husband. Then he's away so much of the time—the Admiral, I mean. It isn't as if they've got much money. They haven't. Gavin will have to do

83

something. And he doesn't seem to realise it. But, then, as she's always given him everything, why should he? So he's really drifting. And if he had been a friend of Pugh's, he would only have taught Pugh to drift, too. So I'm not sorry about that.

It isn't that I dislike Gavin, you understand, but I am sorry for Fanny, even if she has rather brought it on herself. Because she was a girl with real possibilities, too. I can't think why she married that stick, Blair Summers. It's thrown her into a conventional world which she's a cut above, really.

Gavin takes after *her*. There's nothing of his father in him. She was clever when she was young, and all over the place, like him. She used to scandalise society. Not by anything actual, I don't think. But just by not being dull and conforming, but taking the lead in any mischief that was going, and by speaking up and having opinions which girls weren't supposed to. I always heard from the grown-ups that she was 'awful', and I accepted that. I was frightened of her boldness. She was actually much more daring than her sister, so that it's odd that her sister married so much better. I suppose the men of the time were rather frightened or put off by Fanny's unconventionality, and so she got rather left out and took Blair Summers *faute de mieux*.

Not that you'd call her unconventional now—she's horrified by my Socialism and we really don't meet much. But you can see she was—unconventional, that is—in her way, at the time; and it led nowhere. And so Gavin seems to have inherited that from her. All his qualities are leading nowhere.

It's a pity, I think, that he doesn't interest himself in politics—Gavin I mean. Like his brother. He's so intelligent he must see the way things are going and how serious it's all getting, and how absolutely necessary a change is. I know boys like those are isolated from a first-hand knowledge of it all by their wretched education. It's the same with Pugh. They become just echoes of their Master's voices. Why, do you know, Pugh actually said to me about those millions of wretched unemployed that they could easily find work if they wanted to? It's the sort of thing his step-father says! I fairly told him off. He ought to try feeding a family on the miserable little scrap of a dole which is all they get! I told him . . .'

'But Gavin would never talk like that,' I interrupted.

No, Gavin wouldn't. That's true, I suppose. But he doesn't care any more than Pugh does. If he cared, he would have to do something about it, and he wouldn't be so unhappy about himself. I blame Gavin much more than Pugh. Pugh with his reactionary background hasn't had the chance of knowing really. But Gavin has. After all, his uncle may not be as advanced as he could be. But he's not a total reactionary like David. He's a Liberal, and Gavin must often have heard these things discussed rationally down at Shaw Wood. I myself have heard Sir George damning this so-called National Government for their wanton disregard both for the unemployment problem and their kow-towing to Hitler. Gavin must have heard it often. He could be alive to it if he wanted to be. He's just thoroughly self-centred.

GAVIN'S FILE III

[Martin found Gavin a very interesting character.]

He's what Harry might well have been, Martin said, if Harry had had the same chances in life. Like Harry, he can make something of the moment as it passes (though they do it in different ways, I agree) and, like Harry, he has no

85

ability to plan beyond it. It is as if nothing the future has to offer either of them is at all acceptable, and they try to live completely shut off in the present.

But Gavin is what Harry isn't, a very tough character. Make no mistake about that. Anyone who thinks of Gavin as 'sweet' is in for a big shock sooner or later. He has a sweet side, but whenever it comes to the push, you can be sure that toughness will take over.

He's very bitchy—he's very bitchy about me, I know. But on the whole he's very funny with it. Yet I can see that for characters weaker than himself that bitchiness could be very destructive. Both Harry and he are destructive characters. They hate other people being able to live their lives in a way they can't. But if Gavin ever did find something that really engaged him, he'd push his way absolutely ruthlessly to the top.

What he certainly ought to do is get away from that mother of his. His brother Spencer never had any doubt about that. Why Gavin can't is the interesting question. Usually in these mother-bound cases, one has some sense of the ties that bind the boy to the woman. With Gavin one has absolutely none. I've heard him defend even his father, just as he always defends that old arch-Liberal uncle of his if anyone else attacks him.

Have you ever heard him defend his mother? Yet the tie must be there and it must be very strong indeed. Of course, whatever you may think of her, she has got a colossal overdose of personality. She's decidedly a some-body. Is it that, with that passionate emotional flow, she drowns him? Is he unable to compete, and can't escape until he thinks he can? It's obviously a battle of some kind, and Gavin hasn't got the strength to win it. He hasn't really even got the strength to fight it. Has he even the *will* to fight it, full out? The great difficulty for him is that she's able to charm us all. He comes round telling us how awful
86

she is, then we meet her, we fall for her. So he feels without allies.

'Have you ever advised him to leave home?'

Often, and it has no effect at all. You see, Gavin is clever, and he uses all his cleverness to counter any arguments you put up. That is to say, he quite agrees he ought to, and then produces a dozen arguments to show why he won't. Where would he go? What alternatives has he got? Since he's not going to make anything of his life wherever he is, he might just as well stay where he is and be comfortable, if nothing else. And so on and so on. All adduced simply to demonstrate that nothing will make him budge. So there he is, locked in some impotent struggle and absolutely refusing to face whatever it is, indeed using all his cleverness not to discover the reasons, but to keep them in being. Poor Gavin. And, of course, too, he's quite aware that there's somewhere in that situation the little-boy-lost angle that appeals to people. So that they can call him 'sweet', and, though he pretends to dislike that, he uses it all the same, to get his way.

'You see a lot of him?'

A good deal. He had this sort of affair with Harry, you know, though I think it was all on his side. But he drops in a good deal, and one tries to help. But nihilism like his is really impossible to argue with. His is really rather horrifyingly complete. He simply can't see the point in anything at all. He could obviously get a First at Oxford, if he worked. But then, he'll argue, who wants a First anyhow? What satisfaction will that give him? And if he doesn't feel there's any satisfaction in it, one can't make him. He's writing this autobiographical novel and has shown me bits. They're very lively and acute. But I can't persuade him to go on with it. He says he has nothing to write about because nothing ever happens to him. Make something happen, I tell him. How, he says? And he told me what a morning was like for him. A desolation of nothingness. Poor Gavin! One can't really help him.

GAVIN'S FILE IV

[Extracted from Gavin's novel.]

A DEMO

At Victoria Gavin took the Underground to the Embankment. It was a sultry August day: many of the other passengers wore open-necked shirts as if they were going to take advantage of the sun in the parks. At various stations along the route, he noticed other people going for the same purpose as himself, some carrying furled banners or flags, some wearing devices in their button holes, or little red flags with UNITY printed along them in gold letters.

There were already signs of the demonstration at Westminster. Extra police—tough, heavy, indifferent, with rolled mackintoshes—more UNITY badges, more banners and flags. When he emerged from the station the skeleton of the procession was already formed along the Embankment itself—as long a one as he remembered seeing; it stretched right out of sight towards Charing Cross.

Here there were mounted police and officials on motorcycles moving up and down marshalling the people. Red flags, and a whole variety of Trade Union banners and makeshift slogans streaming out on the gentle wind. Along the length of it there was an air of holiday-making, shouts were exchanged, greetings and jokes, which made the massed police seem otiose, even slightly ridiculous. Along the pavements moved sellers of papers, pamphlets, badges, chewing-gum and chocolate.

Gavin walked down the ranks looking for the banner

88

which would mark Harry's district. When he found it, Harry was not there; he didn't like to join it without an introduction; so he stood for a moment on the pavement, feeling awkward, shut out, wishing he belonged to some organisation so that he should be really a part. Not outside. Why wasn't Harry there?

When Harry had rung up and suggested his coming, Gavin had been less short than usual. He had never really fallen for the current political enthusiasm, even rather resented his friend's absorbtion in it; and usually did his best to sabotage it by ridicule; but—and this increased his vexation by a kind of geometrical progression—always without success. Today, however, was Sunday; and Sunday in London he considered one of the drabbest institutions which a drab civilisation had invented—so that it almost seemed as if the English, a guilt-ridden race, had to punish themselves for taking holidays. By comparison with anything else that Sunday offered, a demonstration was exciting, and he had agreed to come.

He walked down to the end of the procession which was quickly filling up; it was impressively long; it stretched well past Charing Cross. He remarked to himself—and he enjoyed remarking it—as if it confirmed some damaging impression, while at the same time it relieved him of some responsibility—that they were mostly petit-bourgeois with a sprinkling of intellectuals. They looked like black-coated rather than manual workers.

Harry was there with his section by the time Gavin returned to it, and greeted him, 'Here you are, Gavin. I thought maybe you'd decided not to come.' He introduced him to the others immediately around: a fat-faced, smiling man in a neat blue suit and rimless glasses, Jane, a serious girl with severely parted dark hair, and a boy of eighteen who carried one pole of a banner. 'This is Gavin. He's going to march with our section. Is that all right?' They received

89

him with friendliness and talked while they waited for the march to begin. *It was a good demonstration. Yes, wasn't it? There must be five thousand here. More like ten. It was going to be hot marching. Wished they hadn't brought coats. What were the slogans to be?* Somebody knew; they practised them.

HANDS OFF US (pause)—HITLER
WORKERS OF THE WORLD UNITE
HELP THE GERMAN WORKERS FIGHT

What was the latest news from Germany?
Anyone heard?
There was a lot of coming and going of the mounted police and the marshalls on their motor-cycles. Presently the sound of bugles and drums came faintly down from the top and the procession moved off.

Marching was quite fun: and singing especially. Watching Harry out of the corner of his eye, Gavin was aware of some irritation at the extreme seriousness which he gave to it, striding along, very conscious of being a unit in the march, integrated and solid, shouting the slogans in time with others, or singing, leading the rest.

England, Arise, the long, long night is over:
Faint in the East, behold the dawn appear!

But an officious marshall hurried back from two files ahead and ordered them not to sing until he gave the word.

'That's pretty intolerable,' Gavin remarked.

'Discipline, Comrade Summers, discipline,' Harry said half ironically, but with enough conviction to annoy him. 'Remember we're the Party of discipline.'

In Victoria Street the marshalls allowed them to sing— the Internationale. The long procession wound down the whole length of the street, stretching further than could be seen in front or behind. The street was empty of traffic, only a few by-standers, some amused, many indifferent, a few enthusiastic, paused to watch them.

On the left and right the shops and solid business houses with their pretentious dead façades served as a sounding board for the song, so that 5,000 voices caught between the metal road and the stubborn pillared fronts ricocheted from side to side, magnifying the militancy of the song's stresses. And a warm emotional flow from the marching, the singing, the united feet, the echoed and re-echoed voices ran along the length of the procession, knitting them into an emotional whole, ready at this moment to go wherever, and to do whatever, their leaders wanted.

> Then, Comrades, come rally,
> And the last fight let us face.
> The Internationale unites the Human Race.

Gavin, resisting, stood outside it: he marched, he sang because he liked singing; but as he glanced sideways at Harry swinging, surrendered to the marching beat, a smile of fervour on his lips, and past him at the rest absorbed in the whole, he felt only a vague disgust which turned to anger.

'Where exactly is the difference?' he said to himself, because Harry was far beyond talking to. 'Haven't we already proved this bogus, round the War Memorial, on the touch-line, when we sing God Save the King, the school song? Schoolmasters use it to retard the growth of their pupils. Anyone can create it and use it, and for any purpose, but surely we ought to be beyond it. Don't they realise the danger?'

But the columns swung on past Victoria up Grosvenor Place into Hyde Park, united, integrated into a confident whole by the warm emotional flow of the marching beat and the singing voices.

Gavin's file passed the main platform, a cart, with red

flags at each corner: clenched fists were raised and answered; they wheeled round the demarcation points, past the band in the centre; cheers greeted their banner, they laughed and shouted in reply, came up into their position and halted.

The column fell out; they were all hot and a little tired; they sat down and lighted cigarettes, ate chocolates and furled the banners.

'That went off very well, I thought,' Harry said to Gavin. 'Did you enjoy it?'

'Oh, it was all right,' Gavin agreed. 'What happens now? Speeches, I suppose.'

'We're under a good platform, too,' said Harry, with an enthusiasm the naïvety of which Gavin noted.

After a few minutes' silence Harry talked to someone else. Gavin suddenly said: 'I don't think I shall wait for the speeches.'

'Why not, for God's sake?' Harry was mildly indignant.

'I know exactly what they're going to say. I don't need to hear it all again. I think I'll go off and have some tea.'

'Christ Almighty, Gavin, what's wrong with you?' Harry was genuinely shocked. 'You can't just break away now. The march isn't half over yet. The speeches are going to be very short; then we go on; this is only half way. We're going on to Shoreditch.'

'You never told me that . . . then it won't be over till about seven? I can't possibly wait as long as that anyhow. I've got to be back for dinner.'

'But you can't go off in the middle of a march. You can't just leave it now. It's impossible.'

'Why not? Why can't I? Of course, I can. In fact, I'm going to. Anyhow, it's going to pour with rain in a minute. We'll all get soaked and I haven't a coat.' Indeed, large ominous clouds had already begun to appear. From the platform the voices of the speakers, denunciatory and violent, rose and fell. But only the front ranks could hear them; at the back they could hear the sudden bursts of clapping or the grumbled cries of 'Shame!'

'I've got no coat either,' Harry protested, 'but I'm not going to walk out in the middle. You can't do it, Gavin. You said you'd come on the march, and it looks so bad if people go away before it's over. What would happen if everyone did it?'

'Christ, don't start that.' So it *was* the same. It led them to exactly the same position. It might have been his housemaster speaking. '*Of course you can't leave the Corps, Summers. What would happen if everyone did it?*' The reverse side of the same medal.

'If everyone did it, Harry, there'd be no march; but then why should there be, if *no one* wants it?'

'But we do want it; of course we want it, don't be silly, Gavin.'

'Well, what are you complaining about? I don't want to get wet myself. But if you want to, I'm not stopping you.'

Already a few large drops were beginning to fall. The speakers were clambering down from the platform; a gust of wind swept across the park with a swirl of rain; coats were put on; the onlookers turned and ran towards the trees for shelter. 'I'll meet you at 8.30 outside the Pavilion,' Gavin threw out as a kind of challenge as he turned away. Then he slipped through the re-forming ranks and joined the spectators as the bugles and drums set up a march. He was really black inside with indignation as he stood there. To find these arguments being used again, the same underhand appeals to the voluntary compulsion of loyalty, the same mass spirit being carefully worked up, however different the purpose.

The rain was steady and thick, the procession was marching by; the paint running from the banners, the red

93

from a flag staining a girl's dress. But she went on with a visible show of brave indifference, like a limping football player in a house match. 'It's not for the sake of a ribboned coat or the selfish thought of a season's fame . . .' Gavin quoted to himself, as he leant against the wet railing watching the marchers bravely enduring this wetting. 'Where's the difference?'

Now Harry's section. Harry on the outside. Shoulders held deliberately more erect, head higher, a few sheets of the *Daily Worker* across his chest, his hair damp and matted. He saw Gavin, smiled wtih the superiority of suffering, beckoned to him. 'So consciously the Hope of his Side,' Gavin murmured as he turned away making for the Underground.

PART TWO

Letters from Abroad

That summer Martin and Harry found a pleasant seaside place to stay in just outside Dubrovnik. Both Gavin and Nellie joined them from time to time. I was earning my living at this time as a private tutor to backward or disturbed boys and had one on my hands at the time. So that I couldn't accept Martin's generous offer to pay my fare and put me up there. As it was, I have this little collection of letters from them which trace the beginnings of the break-up between Martin and Harry.

FROM HARRY

Before we came here Martin and me were lent this apartment in Vienna by a Viennese woman writer. I liked her very much, as Martin did, too. And I didn't mind Martin trying it out with her. You've got to try everything, haven't you? But it's getting more serious. For one thing, she's a Jewess, you see, and with Hitler creeping closer and closer, they don't know where they are in Austria. They're all scared, as who wouldn't be? She's rather rich and getting her money out, and she'll probably come to England. And I think she's crazy about Martin.

But the thing is, she's coming here first. *Can you possibly come?* I want to see what you think.

And you'll love it here. It's a little seaside resort outside the town. Very simple and very *cheap*. The beaches are huge, soft sand, and the weather's divine. We lie about all day, and the boys come out from Dubrovnik, and they're all slim and brown or golden and ready for anything. 'Lovely and willing every afternoon.'

And it's easy to get into Dubrovnik by bus and there are lovely fish restaurants.

We feel rather guilty here with all this going on in Europe. What do the papers say? It looks like another success for Hitler in the Rhineland. But it's so lovely: we can't come back yet. *Do* come. I want your advice. You know me and Martin haven't been getting on too well lately. I irritate him. And now with this Elvira coming here, I don't know. Martin talks about us living separately, anyhow. He says he'll get me a flat in Bloomsbury somewhere. Do come. . . . You know he trusts you and you could talk.

Gavin has been here for a week now. He was rather down in the mouth when he came out but seems to be cheering up at last. I think I'm quite good for him. He thinks too much, and I don't let him. I don't know why he isn't happier than he is. After all he's got everything, looks, brains and money. It ought to be enough to be going on with. Martin says he suffers from *accidie* which is a disease of the soul the monks used to get. But Gavin isn't a monk by any means.

You ought to see him picking his afternoon bed-mate. You know that funny greedy way he has of wanting to gobble up everything in sight, but wanting most of all whatever anyone else wants? He's a funny boy. I don't really get him. He seems so selfish, then does something absolutely surprising, like the other day I was admiring a tie he was wearing, and that evening it was on my dressing table with a little note—a present.

He thinks too much about himself.

Come out and jerk him out of it.

Love,
Harry.

FROM GAVIN

It's a lovely place. You'd love it. It's a bit difficult here, though, with Martin and Harry getting on each other's nerves. It would be a very pleasant diversion to have you here, too.

Harry is just the same, as sweet as ever and just as much on the surface. I'm afraid I no longer think I'm in love with him. It wouldn't have been any good. He's always ready for everything, always agreeable (except with Martin now); he does have this marvellous quality of never having to wonder, what shall I do now? And you never have to wonder while you're with him. He lives in the moment and off the moment. And he does live all the time.

And out here there's very little of that maddening puritanism that came over him when he first joined the Party. That's something I simply can't understand in him. It's so unlike him. Even I got rather bored with it in London, always trying to drag me off to meetings and demos, and simply furious if I didn't go. Martin can't resist twitting him all the time, and there is something comically Victorian about the Party, isn't there, as if they could never escape from the shadow of Karl Marx's beard. Then they live perpetually in a world of bad translationese, all their stuff having been got from the German:

> Arise ye starvelings from your slumbers!
> Arise ye criminals of want!

Could any words be more absurd? 'How is our criminal of want today?' Martin asks Harry in the morning. And over all this Harry loses his sense of humour.

Still, we manage to have golden days and silver evenings. There's an air of unalloyed pleasure hanging over this place, delusive but entrancing. It's a combination of the perfect weather, the perfect bodies, and the distance from all the horrors.

But I never quite get away from those, do you? I mean the horrors of having to decide, having to choose, having to exert the will and not knowing in what direction to do it. That's where Harry is so lucky. Life, decision and choice jet up from some artesian well inside himself. Life for him is really so simple—if only he'd leave it that way—another drink, another boy, another bathe, another expedition. And no regrets, fears, guilt, worries about the future.

I wish I could decide what to do with my life: the indecision is killing me. How does one decide? Pleasure? I get none. Interests? I haven't any. Desire? None. *La chair est froide, et j'ai lu tous les livres.* Is *froide* right? I can't quite remember.

Come and see us.

Gavin.

FROM MARTIN

Can't you really come out and join us here? It's a beautiful little spot we've found, very near Dubrovnik and yet completely remote. Only at weekends they come out from the town to our beaches; otherwise we have them to ourselves, except for the persistent, and by no means uninviting, trade which parades up and down for our delectation. There's a charming orange grove of a garden where I write every morning and life would be ideal, if only . . .

'If only' is the trouble, and I'm sure you could help. You see Harry and I have reached a point where we really mustn't go on living together. It's a sad situation where two people are so dependent on one another as we have become and yet are death to each other. And that's the point we've reached. As long as we are together, I can see absolutely clearly that *he'll never do anything at all.* He is what I suppose ordinary people would call bone idle—or lazy anyhow. But I can see it's not quite that. I'm sure that on his own he might make something of his life, if he was really up against it and had to. But I've corrupted him. He's no longer got the will to do anything as long as I am there to relieve him of the necessity. On the other hand he hasn't any talent for living without doing anything. I know you all think he has, and that's one of his great merits—his ability to live day by day. But that's deceptive. When you're all around, he takes his colour from you. He can be the very spirit of the holidays. But when you aren't, he's left flat and can't even fill his days.

If I had a lot of work for him to do, it might be different. But as you know, I work very slowly, and all the time I'm working I can feel him resenting it, and I have to make the effort to put myself outside the circle of his resentment before I can begin, and it's too much. I've turned him into a drone, and in some sort of unconscious revenge he would like to turn me into one. The only possible hope for us is to give up living together. This makes him very unhappy even though he may—as I think he does—know it to be true. I'm going to get him a separate flat when we get back and see what happens then. Do come out and help us. We need reassurance. I, that it's the right thing to do; he, that if it does happen I shall still love and cherish him.

Love,
Martin.

Well, I got here with great difficulty! Would you believe it! I lost all my luggage somewhere on the platform at Trieste and *all* my money was in the small suitcase. So there was I on this divine boat sailing down the Adriatic—and how beautiful it is—without more than a ten-shilling note and few coppers. It was all right at first. I had enough for a drink and the blue sky and the sun and the placid, flashing water were enough in themselves. You join the boat in the morning and it goes down the coast all day and night and arrives the next morning.

I didn't mind going without lunch, it was all so lovely to look at. But I *was* hungry by dinner-time. My mouth watered when the steward came round ringing the bell! And as I didn't move, he came and asked if I wasn't having dinner? So I explained, and they were charming. He took me to the Captain and he looked at my passport, and when he saw I was English said, couldn't I give them a cheque? Well, I did have my cheque book, and they took my cheque just like that. Wasn't it trusting of them? I might have been anybody. So I got dinner and a cabin and everything. And my bags came on later untouched. These are a peasant people, you see, and left to themselves, they have all the virtues of peasantry. A natural good nature and kindliness for those in trouble. It's only their rulers who corrupt them.

You can't help noticing how corrupted they are under their Fascist King. There's an awful lot of poverty in Dubrovnik itself, and it seems to be decaying slowly. This gives it a certain picturesque romantic air. But it's easy for us to drop out here and enjoy that, isn't it? But the poverty everywhere is terrible.

The little place Martin and Harry have found is *so* nice. It's all delightfully simple but clean and good, the little hotel. The beach is beautiful and the bathing lovely, but you see the underlying corruption in the young men who come out, looking for German women, Martin says, who pay them highly for their services. You can't blame the boys—they're so poor here.

There is rather a feeling of strain between Harry and Martin and I'm so glad I came because Harry can pour his heart out to me. Martin had invited an Austrian woman. I must say she *was* very fascinating—I only had one evening with her. She's a writer, and a member of a Socialist group who are 'underground'. It's very dangerous in Vienna now and they operate partly from Czecho-slovakia. But the régime is very brutal if they're caught, and besides that there's always the danger of Hitler swooping, which they think he'll do at any minute now. I must say I did envy her, though. The life they all lead is intensely dangerous. But it's *real*. She is probably coming to England and I shall take her to see that ass of a brother of mine. Perhaps someone who has gone through all she has gone through may be able to convince him of the real dangers of the Nazis. The trouble with people like David, and all of them, is that they never get anywhere near the places where the pressure is being put on. I suppose they get dispatches and so on, but they don't believe them. If he had been here, listening to her describe what happened to friends of hers, surely he'd be bound to realise how explosive the situation is. I suggested my going to Vienna if there was anything I could do. But she said that we could help best from outside. I felt so ineffectual, and rather guilty, enjoying ourselves here in this Fascist strong-hold, while they are fighting, really fighting, just up there.

Harry is naturally rather jealous of her and the future for him and Martin looks rather uncertain. But I think it's a comfort for Harry to have someone to talk to.

Love, Nellie.

103

I wish you had been able to come. I shall have to leave, I can see. I'm between two devils with the deep blue sea not quite compensation enough. Martin and Harry are now in such a state that they can hardly talk to each other. Martin has definitely decided to set Harry up in a flat of his own, and Harry simply won't accept the decision. There's no one so stubborn as Harry when he has to do something he doesn't want to, and all the airiness has gone out of the holiday.

I try to keep out of it but, of course, I can't. First one, and then the other, gets me on one side and explains how beastly the other is. I take no sides. I just agree. Everyone is beastly. I'm beastly. I just hate them quarreling and spoiling everything.

For this place is really a sort of earthly paradise. What more could one possibly want (except life, except life, except life!) than the ideal temperature, cheap but delicious food and totally uninvolved love every afternoon?

If only people wouldn't get involved! If only they could take love as the boys take it, pocketing it together with their pound! And what boys! Nellie with whom I have over-lapped was wonderfully shocked by them and attributed their lack of morals to the Fascist King. I suppose it is rather shocking that our varied enjoyment depends so largely on unemployment. At least I dare say it does. But I also think that the Adriatic climate does wonders in loosening the moral fibre. The happy thing is they thoroughly enjoy it.

Really this place spoils one for anywhere else, and if you want picturesque architecture you just drop into Dubrovnik, and if you want romantic scenery, you take a trip into the mountains. We did the other day, and rounding one of the hairpin bends we were held up by a convoy of military cars.

And do you know who was sitting, fat, upright and sleek, in the back seat of the first? Göring in person!

You may well imagine what a political frisson it gave Martin and Harry. It drew them together for quite half an hour. As for me, I just saw a fat slug-like thing in a uniform. No, I'm lying. It was frightening. It suddenly brought the horror terrifyingly close. For, of course, I do feel the horror like everybody else—coming closer and closer and closer. I just don't deceive myself into thinking I can do anything to prevent it. Why, I can't even decide which of two things I want for lunch, much less how to run the world. In fact I think, in spite of the domestic horror, I shall stay on here simply because if I don't, what should I do?

How weary, flat, stale and unprofitable seem to *you* all the uses of this world?

Gavin

FROM NELLIE

I think you really ought to make an effort to come out here, if you can. Both Martin and Harry think that you might somehow be able to do something to compose their differences. Which are very bad at the moment. They hardly speak to each other. And I don't know what to say. I think there is something to be said for Harry's living on his own for a bit, anyhow. I don't see any other solution, though I think Martin is being rather selfish over it. He tries to persuade himself that he's doing it for Harry's good. But that doesn't wash with me. He wants to be free to live his own life and feels Harry is in the way.

But Harry isn't a selfish person. He's talked to me a lot and says he wouldn't interfere with Martin if Martin wanted to see much more of Elvira, which he does. And I don't think he would—Harry, I mean, interfere. He's much too fond of Martin for that. And though he's a much more independent person than Martin realises, it is rather hard after three years being pushed out into the cold. And there's so much he can do for Martin. For one thing he can keep him, by example, more on the line.

Actually I think this Elvira has been very good for Martin. It's brought him into touch with someone who is actually in the fight, right there in it, and who knows consequently that one can't dither between alternatives. Those Vienna Socialists are in the very front line, and they can't be asking themselves all the time whether or not what they are doing is betraying some abstract principle or other. The enemy is clear, and so is the way of fighting him.

It's easy enough for me to talk, of course, I agree, sitting here in the sun in this delightful setting in a country that is, anyhow on the surface, peaceful. I feel rather guilty about it half the time with Martin and Harry spending so much energy on a purely private quarrel and Gavin doing nothing at all but wallow in his indecision. He makes me very impatient—Gavin, I mean. What has he got to complain about when only forty miles away from us they are fighting for their lives and their freedom? And he is greedily able to enjoy all the pleasures that this lovely spot offers. He might at least be content with that. I come home tomorrow and must really make up my mind what I am going to do about the Party.

But it isn't quite so easy as I thought. Elvira and her friends are none of them Party members. But they fight just as hard, and, as a matter of fact, though I didn't quite understand why, they don't entirely trust the Party. She said you couldn't, though I should have thought the Party fought hardest of all. Yet no one could fight harder than these Socialists. She seemed to think that if the Party had their way, they would simply throw in their lot with the USSR. And I should have thought that that would be the

very best thing. But she and her friends want above everything their independence, when it's all over. And she
seemed to think that the USSR wouldn't allow it. But
isn't the USSR fighting for the independence of the working classes everywhere in the world? And wouldn't alliance
with the USSR make them stronger? Harry argued with
her a lot. But I didn't feel so inclined to. After all she,
Elvira I mean, was in the thick of it and ought to know.
What I feel is it's a very great pity that there should be these
divisions. After all we want the same thing really, the
overthrow of Fascism and an end of exploitation and the
threat of war. Logically both Socialists and Communists
have the same objective. The French Popular Front is
surely showing us the way, united against the common
enemy. But the fact that Elvira and her friends, there in the
thick of it, don't really trust the Communists is very
worrying to me. Harry, who is more simple-hearted and
straightforward, was sure she was wrong. I couldn't be so
certain.

Love,
Nellie.

FROM MARTIN

I think that, at last, after weeks of arguing and disagreeable-
ness, Harry has at last accepted the situation and agreed to
go into a flat on his own when we get back. Has he written
to you? I'd love to hear what he says about it to a third party,
so do write if you hear from him. I'm really sure it will be
better for him, and know it will be for me. I met in Vienna
this fascinating woman writer, Elvira. She'll be over in
England in a month or two, and I so want you to meet her.
She's a member of the anti-Fascist Front here, which means
working underground.

And I must say it's a kind of a shock to find all the things I saw going on in Germany going on there too. The fact is we are absurdly cushioned from the realities in comfortable, safe, blind old England. All our political dilemmas and questionings and wonderings are a sort of make-believe game. It doesn't make the slightest difference really, back there, whether I join the Communist Party or call myself a Socialist or just go on writing my novels. But there, in Vienna, such decisions are matters of life and death, or at least imprisonment. And she and all her friends are having to take decisions like that every day.

I must say I think it would do Gavin the world of good to have to live in that sort of atmosphere for a bit. He's our problem, now. He simply cannot make up his mind what to live for or what to live *about*.

I think that it's this failure of belief which is the prevailing malaise of the time. Half England is afflicted with it. As long as people live in some inherited or accepted pattern, it doesn't reveal itself; the routine and the conventions carry them along. But the moment they are, for some reason, jerked out of that, the disease takes hold. They find they are empty and feel they're useless.

But it's really desperate with someone as intelligent and such fun as Gavin is, or can be. He ought to have gone home weeks ago, but he lingers on because he has nothing to go home *for*. Here at least there is a pattern of pleasure shaped by the weather, the ambience and our gentle routine. It just keeps him going—but only just. And in the evening he's inclined to fall into a deep melancholy out of which we can't shake him. It's a shame, isn't it, for anyone so gifted to disbelieve so completely in their gifts? Let me know if you hear from Harry.

Love,
Martin.

Well, Martin and me have come to an understanding. I'm to try living on my own for six months and then we review the situation. You might look around Bloomsbury for me and see if you can hear of any nice flats going. I don't want anything posh. Just two bedrooms and a sitting-room, cheap but airy. Do you know I'm quite looking forward to it? It'll be fun to come back to. I'm pretty sure it won't last, actually. I think Martin needs me, even if he doesn't notice it now. But he'll see what it's like when I'm not there. And there's something to be said for being on your own. No pressure all the time to get this done, or do the other. Perhaps I may get a job, too. Only I mean to devote much more time to the Party. You could see from the way Elvira talked about Vienna how serious everything is getting. We've got to work very hard if we're to save anything, and after this lovely holiday, I'm ready to get down to it.

Because it has been lovely, in spite of Martin and me bickering. That's just part of a relationship, isn't it? And now it's all settled I feel fine. I wish we could find someone for Gavin, I really do. I'm sure that's what he needs, a nice cosy affair, then he'd stop thinking so much about himself. I'm going to make it my business when I get back to fix him up. You'll see, it will make all the difference.

We'll be back in a week or so, but it'll be very hard to leave. I feel this is the last of those lovely sunny carefree holidays before it all explodes. There's a funny sort of feeling in this country that it can't go on, that these are the last days of a dying era. For, of course, we may have laughed at Nellie when she kept saying it, but there is something corrupt here. It's in the atmosphere. I say, enjoy it while one can. It wouldn't do any good not to, would it? But it couldn't go on. Half our pleasure comes from the cheapness and that means poverty for them, and unemployment and everything. Sooner or later the boil will burst and I'm afraid it'll be sooner rather than later.

So we're making the best of it while it lasts. Even Gavin is. The awareness of it coming to an end sort of sharpens the appetite. It's a shame you haven't been able to come. You'd have loved it all: and now we know where we are we can revel in the last week. We're all relaxed again and happy.

Look out for that flat for me.

Love,
Harry.

PART THREE

Enter Pugh

In July 1936 the Spanish War broke out. The Generals in Spanish Morroco organised a revolt against the Popular Front Government and, though the situation was very confused, it soon looked as if a full-scale civil war was raging. Madrid, held by the Government, was under siege. Most of the western half of the country seemed to be in the General's hands, and the Spanish Fascists, the Falange, were naturally supporting the rebellion.

But the Government was fighting back and seemed to be winning in the middle, in the north and in Catalonia. For us, at the start of it, there was practically no other topic of conversation. To us the issue seemed as clear as anyone could possibly want. The Spanish Popular Front Government had been elected by democratic processes and was clearly entitled to receive every support. The Generals' rebellion was obviously Fascist-inspired. Here was the whole European issue at its most naked and pure, Democracy versus Fascism.

But it soon became clear that this was not to be the generally accepted view in ruling-class quarters. The Tory press justified the revolt on the grounds that the elections were not valid and that the Popular Front had not been able to establish order. Much play was made on both sides with atrocities committed before the revolt and in its first few weeks.

But we supposed—and argued—that France's Popular Front Government under Blum would have to give all support to the Democratic Government of Spain and that our Government would have to follow suit, however reluctantly. Already the Dictators, Hitler and Mussolini, had declared themselves for the rebel Generals and were rumoured to be sending arms and technicans to help them.

113

Now, by International Law an elected Government was entitled to get arms from where it could to defend itself, and the Spanish Government asked for these from us; yet both France and England seemed to be hesitating. Finally, under Blum's initiative, they convened a Non-Intervention Committee which both Hitler and Mussolini agreed to join, which would see that no arms went to either side. The Committee would 'hold the ring'. With characteristic duplicity Hitler and Mussolini, in spite of having seats on the Committee, simply continued barefacedly to send supplies and, finally, troops, while the French and English, with characteristic timidity, shut their eyes to these facts and refused the Spanish Government any assistance at all. It was left to Russia, who was also a member of the Committee, to send some arms and technicians, though she never sent them in anything like the quantities the Dictators did.

All the same, the Spanish Government survived and seemed to be holding its own. In England the result of these events was to sharpen up all political activity and to drive an even deeper wedge between the Left and the Right. As far as we were all concerned we were drawn yet further into politics. Gavin's brother Spencer joined up with the International Brigade, being recruited to fight on behalf of the Spanish people. This Brigade, though organised by the Communists, was not at the beginning a purely Communist force. To it flowed all the more adventurous of the many refugees from European Fascism and many other idealistic young men from the democracies. And everyone of us wondered whether he, too, shouldn't join it.

Martin gave more and more of his time to political activity instead of writing, and got more and more involved in the inconsistencies which this produced. Harry, who had got rather slack with his attendance at his Cell, returned to it with renewed ardour for at least a month. Nellie could hardly any longer bear to go the Boltons, for it simply meant the swopping of atrocity stories; for, naturally, her Catholic family were all pro-Franco, Franco having become the leader of the revolt and having proclaimed it a religious crusade. As Nellie put it: 'They (the family) assert that we burn churches and nuns, and as I know *for a fact* that we don't, what's the good of going to see them?' Gavin was especially put out that his younger brother had once again stolen a march on him by joining up and didn't know whether to be more proud of him, or envious.

I'm rather surprised to find less about the Spanish War than I had expected in this section. But it must be presumed to be preoccupying our political thoughts though, as always happens, private life had its claims too. And in our circle just at this time the private life of each of us was affected by the arrival in London of young Pugh Griffiths. Without being a particularly remarkable character in himself—except for his looks and his sexual attraction—he managed to disrupt to a greater or lesser degree Martin, Gavin, Nellie and Harry, and was finally the catalyst whose actions resulted in the exodus to Spain. His actual arrival was related to me by Harry, who was now living on his own in a small three-roomed flat in Bloomsbury, and this had turned out only a semi-success. Harry quite liked it, he liked the independence and having no one to chivvy him. All the same, as I recall, he hadn't cut off from Martin very completely. On the contrary, Martin complained that the break had changed too little, and that Harry had only grafted his new life on to the old. He got up later in the morning, but then when he was ready, he simply went round to Martin's, which wasn't very far away, 'just to see what was going on or if he could be any help', and sat about sometimes all day, just as he used to, playing the gramophone and getting in the way.

With Pugh's arrival Harry, at first, spent much more time at his own flat nattering with Pugh.

I had decided to open a file on Pugh and Harry's account of his arrival is the first item, which I see I have rather written up:

PUGH'S FILE I

It was the telephone that had woken him, Harry said. He had reached over and glanced at his watch as he picked up the receiver. 10.30 a.m. Well, he couldn't complain, then. But he made his 'hello' as sleepy as he could to discourage the other voice, which refused to be discouraged.

'Is that you, Harry?'

'Yes, who is it?'

'Pugh!'

'Pugh? Who's Pugh?'

'You know me. I'm Lady Nellie's nephew.'

'Oh yes. What is it, Pugh?'

'Can I come round and see you? It's urgent.'

'Yes, of course. Come along round. You know the way?'

'No.'

I gave him the directions, Harry said, and then got myself up. Quite excited I was. I'd met Pugh with Nellie, of course, and rather fancied him. He was exciting and an awfully good-looking boy, rather too toffee-nosed, if you see what I mean, but promising material.

So I made myself some tea and a couple of pieces of toast like I always did in the morning, had a quick wash and shaved carefully, and I was still hesitating over the choice of a shirt when the doorbell rang. I was alone in the flat luckily, and, pulling on a dressing-gown, went down to answer the door.

Young Pugh was there looking very posh and correct in conventional clothes and turning up his nose slightly at the district. Well, it is rather dishevelled, isn't it, with its milk bottles uncollected on doorsteps, and those children playing at the street corners.

'What a place to live,' was Pugh's greeting.

Well, I wasn't put out. I wasn't going to worry about his stuck-upness. 'What's wrong with Bloomsbury?' I said. 'Everyone lives in Bloomsbury. You can do what you like here.'

'Let's go in,' young Pugh had said, wrinkling his nose.

'Upstairs,' I said, and I noticed his look of upper-class disgust at the worn linoleum, that broken strut in the bannister, and the slightly musty smell. But once inside the first-floor flat, it was cheerful and gay, though I say it myself. The sitting-room is lined with Martin's surplus books, there's the Finnish table covered with papers, the windows are those long Georgian ones, and I'd got some curtains in gay stripes.

'Coffee?' I offered him.

'Yes, please,' and before I went in to make it I put a record on, a Cole Porter song that I thought would cheer him up.

Then I wondered what on earth he was doing here. Wasn't it still term time?

'Yes,' he said, 'it is.'

'Half-term holidays, then?' I suggested.

'We don't have half-term holidays,' he said, in his most class-superior voice.

'That's a rotten sort of school, then,' I told him. I wasn't going to be put down by him. I'm used to that sort of thing. 'What's up, then?'

'I've been sacked.'

I wasn't surprised. Last time I met him Pugh had hinted at the goings-on at school. He seemed to have had a fair old time, and was bound to be found out sooner or later. I asked what it was this time, and he came out with it, trying to shock me, I think. 'Young Jenkins. He was the school tart. And as he had his trousers down and I had mine open, there wasn't much to be said in our defence.' He didn't know what he was going to do now, but he was determined not to go home. I suggested his Aunt Nellie, but he didn't like that idea either. She was too anti-family in a different way. You see, Pugh wasn't a bit ideological like her. He was just a sort of rebel without any reason, always up against authority. Perhaps just a natural dare-devil. Anyhow, he didn't think he could stand Aunt Nellie's trying to enlist him all the time for the Cause.

'Well, you can stay here, if you want to,' I told him. 'There's a spare room.'

And he showed his first signs of being pleased. 'Could I, just while I look around?'

I told him, sure, and showed him the room. It was quite nice really, simple, you know—just a bed and a chest of drawers and a chair, and he looked round it disdainfully and said, 'Better than the streets, anyway.'

But that was just an act really. He didn't care much about his surroundings, and over a cup of coffee we soon got friendly and he did say, after a bit, that I was the best person he could have come to. And I thought so, too. There'd be no pressure here, none of that judging that would go on everywhere else, and he could look around quietly and see what he wanted to do.

He's a funny boy, though. He told me some horrifying tales about that school of his. Aren't they barbaric, those places? And the Catholic ones worst of all. They have this theory that it doesn't matter how much you hurt the body, so long as you save the soul, and, as Pugh was against them all the time, they whipped him, and whipped him and whipped him. I wonder parents send their boys to a place like that, or boys stay there either. Pugh seemed quite proud of himself, being the most whipped boy in the school. I could do without that record. And, anyhow, what was it all for? He didn't seem to know at all. He was just against them for no particular reason that he could give. He just laughed and said you had to be. 'Even at the expense of all that whipping?' I said. 'Well, who cares?' was all he said. 'And now it's all over.'

Then there was the question of facing his father, who was bound to be told, and I suggested the best thing was to do it through Nellie. So we went round and saw her. She was a bit disappointed, I think, that Pugh wasn't staying with her. But she got over that, and promised him a very decent allowance until he found his feet, so that was all right. And she got on to her brother David and told him what had happened in such a way that it all seemed the school's fault, and told him Pugh would be staying in London and she'd keep an eye on him. She was splendid, I must say, and what with the allowance and everything we'd done a good morning's work.

Pugh didn't care much for the Bookshop crowd when I took him round there. In the first place those poets and intellectuals and Socialists weren't at all his kind of people. Pugh's still very upper-class and intolerant. He looked down his pretty nose at them and wrinkled it, as if to say they smelt, which perhaps they did. But we'll have to knock that nonsense out of him, won't we? He's not going to fit in with us, if he takes that high and mighty line. But it'll need time, of course. When I ragged him about it, he wasn't at all inclined to laugh. He just dismissed them as a scruffy crowd, said the café was plain dirty, and waited impatiently for us to leave.

I guess the Gargoyle's more in his line. I took him round there that first evening. And he seemed thoroughly at home. Anyhow, there he is, staying with me. You must come round and meet him. You'll like him, I'm sure.

Naturally the Spanish War which divided the Left very firmly from the Right played an increasing part in our political lives. By this date the battle was swaying as it seemed to us pretty equally though, in fact, the superiority of the Franco-ists in arms, aircraft and military skill was already beginning to tell. But this was the kind of thing which the propaganda of the time concealed from us. And, in any case, we were so violently partisan that objectivity was out of the question.

It was now common knowledge, too, that Germany and Italy were sending arms, aircraft and troops to Spain in defiance of the Non-Intervention agreement, and though we marched, demonstrated and organised petitions day after day and week after week, they made (to our surprise and indignation—so innocent were we) not a scrap of difference. And I think, in the minds of all of us who were single and free, there was the nagging question—should we not, instead of merely demonstrating, join the International Brigade and fight.

Hence, the Gavin–Pugh set-up, which to us at the time looked like just a love affair, was in fact differently motivated:

PUGH'S FILE II

(a)

It was very mysterious, Harry said, the way Pugh suddenly disappeared. He left without saying anything, or leaving a note, nothing. I just came in one day and he wasn't there and didn't come all that evening, and wasn't there in the morning. I was not very worried. It was quite like him to stay out nights with someone and come back in the middle of the morning. But after two days, I did get a bit anxious. I rang up Nellie and she hadn't seen him, and then I rang up Gavin, and he was there. Gavin was very cagey, which was quite unlike him. He just said Pugh was staying with him for a bit and they weren't going out much.

I was rather hurt. He might at least have left a note. Of course, I knew Gavin had always fancied Pugh; but Pugh hadn't shown any more interest than he showed in any handsome boy around. I was very intrigued. Was this really an affair? Pugh was rather heartless, I always thought. Had he suddenly succumbed? It didn't really seem likely to me. But something was up, and I longed to know what.

I went round to see them, of course. And there they both were, looking very conspiratorial, I thought. They didn't say anything which gave them away. They didn't want to talk much. In fact, they weren't at all pleased to see me. They froze me out finally and I didn't go again. I talked it over with Nellie a lot, but we couldn't decide what they were up to. It really was puzzling. Martin knew nothing. No one knew anything. They didn't ring us up. They didn't come and see us. Perhaps it was an affair; I don't know.

All I do know is that, after a week, Pugh suddenly turned up again. He refused to say anything about his absence. What had they been doing, I asked? Nothing in particular, he said. You can't have been in bed all the time, I said. Why not, he said, and left it at that. But he was in a funny mood all the same. Something had gone wrong, and he was bitter about it. But he wouldn't say what it was. He just drank a lot and was wilder than ever. And got turned out of the Gargoyle again. This time for good, or anyhow until he'd paid his debts there.

As to that mysterious week with Gavin, he never

mentioned it again and refused to have it discussed. And Gavin wouldn't say anything about it either. He just hinted that it had been an affair and now was over, and though he saw Pugh quite a bit, I guess he was upset at it ending. So I suppose that's what it was. And poor Gavin got his fingers burned again. He's quite right—he doesn't have much luck, does he?

PUGH'S FILE II

(b)

[*Gavin admitted having had an affair with Pugh during this week, and explained the whole thing, swearing me to secrecy.*]

'Was your affair a success?' I asked Gavin.

It depends what you call a success. You see, Pugh hadn't much heart, I'm afraid. There was this one week when I thought it was going to be much more than just the going to bed together which seemed to satisfy him. We had met a lot and gone out in the evening together, and something seemed to click between us. The thing was that all the others were too intense for him. He was flattered by Martin's attentions, of course. And he found Harry a very amiable companion, as Harry could be, when he wasn't pushing his Communism down your throat. But just at this time he was, rather; and nothing bored Pugh more than that.

Actually at this time Pugh was getting a little bored with London and doing nothing, and he came to me with a suggestion:

'Why don't we go to Spain together?'

It was that 'together', of course, that was the immediate attraction for me. I was falling for him hard, I realised, and the prospect of doing something adventurous like this with him was very exciting. In any case the idea of going to Spain had been at the back of my mind—at the back of all our minds, I think—ever since the beginning, and Spencer's going. (Actually that hadn't worked out. They soon discovered that Spencer was under age and wouldn't risk his being killed. So he had been sent off doing various reporting jobs which he had made a success of, and then had gone off to America, no one knew quite what for.) Anyhow, as I say, the idea had been there in my mind and I was over eighteen. But Pugh wasn't, and didn't look anything like it. But he brushed that aside, and said he was sure he could work it. So we discussed the idea and I got thoroughly excited. The more I thought of it, the more it seemed the very solution. I suppose the thing is I couldn't have contemplated it by myself, but doing it with someone else, and with Pugh of all people in the world, made it perfectly practicable.

We talked about it all that morning and had lunch together on it, and worked ourselves into the mood where we were ready to act, and decided over the coffee that we would go round that very afternoon to enlist. So we got into a taxi, but went to Belgrave Square! And it was only then that I realised that we had been at cross purposes. We had been talking about it only in terms of the adventure, and of getting away from our families. I had naturally assumed that he was thinking of joining the International Brigade, but he wasn't thinking of anything of the sort. He was wanting to join the Carlists, who were a sort of aristocratic branch of Franco's Fascists!

Well, of course, as soon as I realised that, I refused to go in with him, and we went back home for another long wrangle. His argument was childishly simple and rather sweet. 'But the Carlists,' he said, 'wear such lovely clothes! Red berets and a red cloak! Marvellous!' He simply had no feelings about the issues at all, except that he vaguely felt that on the Loyalist side he'd be with a lot of people like the Bookshop crowd, while with the Carlists he'd be with his own sort. When I tried to persuade him to join the International Brigade instead, he admitted, what he hadn't told me before, that he had already put his name down at the Franco Embassy and meant to go on with it. Besides, as he said, the International Brigade wouldn't take him when still under eighteen, while the Carlists, he had found out, didn't mind that. He wasn't going to risk being turned down by the Communists for being too young. All that he wanted was to go. So it was the Carlists or nothing for him. And he begged me to go with him. He was absolutely set on this and nothing else, and I was put on the spot.

He was very insistent, and wheedled and coaxed me, and it was almost impossible to resist him. But I had to. I'm not absolutely sure that I would have, if I'd been quite on my own. I know when I asked myself whether I was really so set on supporting the Republic that I would give Pugh up for it, I found I wasn't. Don't get me wrong. Of course, I knew that all Right was on the Republican side, intellectually. I agreed with everything everyone said about it. But I had no passion for it, no passion that could compare with my growing passion for Pugh. On the other hand I hadn't got the guts, I suppose it was, to commit an act of betrayal to all of you. That's what it would have amounted to, and in the end I couldn't see myself doing it. I very nearly did, I admit. But it seemed too risky. Supposing anything had gone wrong between our committing ourselves and our getting out there, I couldn't have faced you all, and it all seemed very uncertain. We argued all that night. I'd arranged directly we formed the plan that morning that Pugh should come and stay.

My mother—as you can imagine—was delighted to

welcome someone like Pugh. He was just her kind of boy, the sort she would have liked us to be. She made a great fuss of him and gave him Spencer's old room on the top floor next to mine, so we could spend the night together with no one knowing. You can imagine how hard it was to resist him.

But in the end I had to, and we reached a compromise. I would help him all I could to go by himself, if he wanted to. He could stay with me till it was arranged and we'd keep out of the others way. He didn't take it very seriously that Martin, Harry, and Nellie would be horrified by this action and would regard it as a betrayal. He didn't care that much, but he saw the point that they might try to stop him, and agreed that we should keep it secret from them. And another advantage was that staying with me he could have his correspondence addressed to our house, so no one else could know.

The advantage to me was that I would have him all to myself for an indefinite period, and so I did, though it turned out to be a miserably short one.

Anyhow, I went with him to the Carlist headquarters in Belgrave Square. It was all rather grand—frock-coated flunkies and all that—and very unlike the shabby Republican Embassy. He was taken upstairs to some room and interviewed, while I waited downstairs; and he came out again bubbling with excitement. It was all fixed up. He might be off in a week.

He was frightfully grateful for my support, so we had a rather marvellous week, while he was waiting to hear. Of course he had an absolutely crazy, romantic idea of what it would be like. He didn't seem to be able to see it in any realistic terms of actually fighting and perhaps being killed, but only in terms of swaggering round in his red beret and scarlet cloak. I'm not sure he was right about the cloak, anyway.

What I am sure of was that he was in a state of high excitement, and we had this rather marvellous time. By now, of course, I'd fallen about as far in love as you could fall. And I thought what extraordinary and unusual luck it was for me having this beloved creature around with me all day and every day, and every night as well. I didn't quite deceive myself that he was in love with me, too. But he gave quite a good imitation of it. What he was in love with, I suppose, was this idea of going to Spain and, as I was the only person in on it, I got all the glitter and the gaiety of it for myself.

What was typical of me and my situation was that the affair was doomed in this way by time. Well, all affairs are in some sense. 'At my back I always hear . . .' But this one so rigidly and with such a tiny span. I couldn't bear it. I couldn't bear the thought that within a week, a mere week, it would come to an end, if he was accepted. While we were arguing about not letting the others know, because if we did they might put a stop to it, the idea had occurred to me that, if it came to the worst, I could probably put a stop to it myself. His Aunt Nellie was, of course, the answer. She could almost certainly dish it by telling his step-father and getting it stopped officially. So, as that enchanting week went on, it was constantly in my mind that I could use her, if it became necessary. I told myself that it was madness for this divine boy to go out and get himself killed in a cause he didn't really believe in. I told myself that he didn't really know what he was letting himself in for, that he was just romanticising the whole thing and would thank me later for stopping him.

But that wasn't it, really. I just couldn't bear to lose him. So I used to get up before him in the morning and slip down to see what was in the post. Sure enough, it came on exactly the seventh day, an envelope, marked 'The Spanish Embassy'. I took it down to the kitchen in the

127

basement and steamed it open with a kettle. And there was the fatal news. He had been accepted. He was to report in a week's time.

Even then I wasn't certain what to do. Should I just suppress this letter and pretend it hadn't come? Perhaps that would have been best. But I didn't want any suspicion to fall on me. Actually, Pugh was the least suspicious of characters. There was absolutely nothing devious or roundabout in his nature. It was one of his charms. He went straight ahead with whatever impulse dictated at the moment, good, bad or indifferent. He never looked back, he never reflected. All the time I knew him he never made a single generalisation. He never considered what people were like or bore them anything more than temporary ill-will if they had crossed him. In this sense there was something really pure about him. His actions took up the whole of him, there, and only there and then. No past, no future, no comparisons.

Finally I decided—I had to make up my mind quickly—that I'd better let him have the letter, then quietly dish the whole thing. I'm not sure I was right.

The difficulty about steaming open envelopes is how to stick them down again. I made rather a botched job of it, but reckoned he would be so excited that he wouldn't notice. And I was right about that. He was in the seventh heaven when he opened it, which made me feel worse because of what I was going to do.

I had to pretend I was going out to see my doctor, but in fact, I went round to Lady Nellie's. Whether they really knew who he was at the Carlist headquarters or not, I'm not sure. He'd just given his name as Pugh Griffiths, but had taken evidence to show he had been in the OTC, and we had forged a letter as coming from an imaginary father at my address, giving him permission.

But I was pretty sure it could be stopped, his step-father

128

being who he was. And I think I was right to stop it, don't you, even knowing what happened? Though I didn't do it, of course, for that reason.

Lady Nellie was in a terrible state when I told her. Of course she was shocked politically as well. The more so as she really thought she might yet succeed in converting him. Yes, she was in a fine old flap. Her beloved Pugh, recklessly risking his life, and on the wrong side, at that!

I didn't stay long with her. Her flapping always got on my nerves. I just waited for her to ring up her brother, and left her to go off and see him. What happened between her and him, I never discovered. She did ring up rather hysterically later in the morning to tell me that she had failed to get anything done. But that she wasn't going to leave it at that. I just hoped that somehow or other she would manage to get it stopped. Which evidently, in the end, she did.

Meanwhile, when I got back, Pugh was still in a high old state of excitement and I tried to warn him that things might yet go wrong. But when a stern letter came the next day regretting that they had been deceived and cancelling the arrangement, he was beside himself. But there was nothing he could do. He rang up his step-father and began abusing him, but he evidently hung up on him.

He couldn't complain to all the others, because now he didn't want them to know that he had contemplated betraying them. And I had reckoned that this would mean he would have to stay with me. But it didn't work out like that. I'm sure he didn't suspect me of having interfered. He wasn't the sort of person who would try and work things out like that. He just felt that fate was once more against him, and he kicked in every direction. Including mine. And he packed up that very day and went back to Harry; and our affair ended there.

(c)

I blame Gavin, of course, Nellie told me in giving her version. I'm sure he originally put the idea into Pugh's head, and then, I suppose, got cold feet and decided to wreck the scheme. Still, it's no good denying it was terribly irresponsible of Pugh, and we must face the fact that Pugh is just that, thoroughly irresponsible.

When Gavin came round and told me, I could really hardly believe it at first, but when he had persuaded me that it was really true, I rang up David at once, you know, my awful brother, and went straight round to see him. And I had some difficulty in persuading him of the story. He always takes the maddening line now that I'm just an hysterical Lefty and that nothing I say is to be trusted.

Then when at last I got it home to him that I wasn't inventing it—and would have no reason to—he put the tips of his fingers together in that infuriating gesture he has developed when he's being the reasonable, 'wise' statesman and asked, 'Well, come to think of it, why shouldn't he, if he wants to?' Yes, he became quite excited by the idea. The Carlists, you see are extreme Catholics and Royalists, and the idea really appealed to him on those grounds. He's really in his mind given up Pugh as a bad job and this actually—believe it or not—sort of redeemed Pugh in his eyes. If he was prepared to go off and fight the enemy under a Catholic–Royalist banner, he wasn't such a bad lad after all! Yes, it's true! That's how the ruling–class mind really works. Whatever their outward pretence of neutrality, in their heart of hearts the Spanish Government—the legally elected Government—is the enemy, while Franco is a Gentleman cleaning up the Socialists and Communists and Intellectuals. That's how they think, really.

Of course, we were soon in the middle of a violent

argument about this and I couldn't get anywhere with him at first. 'No,' he kept saying, 'I'm disposed to leave things as they are. It won't do the young man any harm. It may even teach him some of the discipline he obviously lacks, and he'll be with a nice crowd, of his own sort. It might be the making of him.'

'A nice crowd, of his own sort!' You see! You see the way their thoughts run? And the fact that this was an extreme, *the most extreme*, group of Fascists out to enslave the Spanish people, meant absolutely nothing to him at all. Didn't he think it would be disastrous, I said, for his name to be associated with such people? And he said, not at all. He'd be quite proud of it, himself. Yes, the boy was showing some spunk at last, and ought to be given his chance.

And he pooh-poohed the idea that it might reflect badly on him as a member of a Government that was supposed to be neutral. 'Besides no one need ever know.' I assured him they soon would know. I'd make it my business to see that they did! And we had another real row about that. But he stuck to his point—he's very obstinate, when he wants to be, David is. 'No,' he said, 'whatever the consequences to me personally—if you insist on dragging our name into the papers—I must think about Pugh, not myself. If he's seriously decided to do this, he ought to be allowed to do it. Mother will agree, I'm sure.'

'And you'll just let him throw his life away?' I said.

'What's he doing now but throwing his life away? If he's going to do that, he might as well do it for something he believes in.'

'Something *you* believe in!' I said furiously. 'Don't imagine that *he* believes in it! He doesn't believe in anything. Why, Gavin told me the only reason he'd picked on the Carlists was because they wore scarlet cloaks and berets!'

'Well, he may come to believe in it,' David said. 'As I see it, it's his big chance. He'll be mixing with decent people, and that'll be a change for the better you must admit. Some of their principles may rub off on him. No, he has my blessing.'

'Mixing with reactionary Fascists and murderers,' I told him, 'that's who you call decent people. Reactionary fanatics of the very worst kind, with no principles but power and suppression. Don't you believe in Democracy any more?'

'Spain is quite different from England,' David said complacently. 'What suits us doesn't necessarily suit them. It's not for us to lay down the law on how they should govern themselves. Democracy has been tried there and has obviously failed, or you wouldn't have decent people like Franco prepared to die to change things.'

Well, it's no use arguing with that kind of thing. So I left him and went home rather despondent. And then later David telephoned and he'd changed his tune. He said that on second thoughts it *would* look rather bad for him as a member of the Government for his son to take sides. Was I determined to get it into the papers if Pugh went? I said I was, and he said he thought I was doing Pugh the greatest disservice I could possibly do him, and one day I'd regret it. I said I'd risk that, and he said he'd see what he could do, and sure enough Pugh's enlistment was cancelled in due course.

I got it out of Mother what actually happened. David consulted some of his colleagues and the Home Secretary himself. They were sympathetic but told him that if Pugh did go, and papers like the *News Chronicle* made a fuss, his position—David's—would be tricky. It would embarrass the Government. He might have to resign. So for all his grand talk about thinking of Pugh before himself, when it came to the point he thought more about himself. Mother said it was the embarrassment to the Government he was thinking of and he was only doing his duty. So like her!

Author's Note

One great event of this period was Martin's affair with Judy, an Oxford undergraduette, and our concern with it was as to how far Pugh had been instrumental in bringing it to an end. It certainly lasted a very short time, and there wasn't any doubt that during it, and during the Oxford term when Judy was in residence, Martin had also carried on what looked like an affair with Pugh.

The dissection and documentation of this event, which I then undertook, seems now, as I read it, rather impertinent, if not actually ghoulish; but in my capacity as a scientific novelist I was at this time blind to such nice considerations. I rummaged around mercilessly for the 'truth':

PUGH'S FILE III

(a)

It was all directed against Harry really, Gavin told me. Having got rid of Harry, Martin had to justify his decision by getting the girl-friend in aid of which the whole process was started. He was justifying himself, don't you see? He had to take the high line of wanting freedom for experiment in order to get Harry off his back with a clear conscience; and, having done that, he had to follow it up by finding the girl, and the wretched Judy was the one chosen for the experiment. And she fell for it.

Yes, I knew her quite well at Oxford in a sort of way. She was one of the few intelligent *and* pretty girls around, and so she had a wide choice. Don't imagine she was an innocent little thing, though. Far from it. I know about four boys that I'm pretty certain she had been to bed with. And she was very attractive. A bit too solemn-serious for me altogether. You know, certain she knew the highest when she saw it, and constantly seeing it. Su-superior, as Lawrence said.

I watched the affair starting when Martin came up to Oxford and found her the intellectual toast of the town. That was the attraction for him, make no mistake. We had a rather quarrelsome meeting at the time. Because I thought he had treated Harry very badly, or anyhow that launching Harry out on his own was a disastrous mistake. And I told Martin so. I told him that Harry was really incapable of this 'standing on his own feet' business, that he wasn't really stable enough and that in due course he would be bound to do something silly, if Martin really cut him off. But Martin wouldn't have it. Said he couldn't be responsible for Harry all his life.

And he came all the heavy stuff with me. You know what he's like in that mood, totally taken up with the great public drama of whether Martin Murray likes women. *How* Martin Murray likes women. *Why* Martin Murray likes women. Why our generation ought to be bi-sexual! The bi-sexual ideal and modern Communism! Forward from Homosexuality! Outward from the single sex! And all that!

And then getting Judy wasn't so difficult for him. If she was the intellectual toast of highbrow Oxford, he, after all, was just the biggest intellectual catch around. There may have been mutual attraction in it, but most of it, I say, was mutual intellectual snobbism. Two big intellectual catches angling for each other. And how Martin adored parading around Oxford with her, snatched from under the noses of all the boys of her own age! I knew that gave him a thrill from the way he used to say deprecatingly to me, did I think he was too old for her? She was only just nineteen, and he was thirty. Was he taking an unfair advantage? Oh yes, as always, he was full of scruples about it all, arguing himself, with all the appearance of scrupulosity, in the direction he meant to go anyhow.

However, I didn't care one way or the other at that time. Let him get Judy, if he could. It did mean, of course, that Harry got pushed further and further out. Because in the two vacs, while it was on, she took up residence with Martin in his flat and got herself paraded around intellectual London. Terribly pleased with herself and he with her, and Harry soon found he was no longer welcome.

Actually, at the time Harry had Pugh staying with him, so he was quite occupied. Still he was very hurt, I know. When I really began to get annoyed was when Judy went back to Oxford and Martin started taking up Pugh. That's typical of Martin, you see. All that guff about heterosexuality, and yet as soon as a pretty boy came along, he was like a bitch on heat again. And if Martin was bad for Harry, he was infinitely worse for Pugh. The whole point about Pugh was that he was a simple upper-class type.

Myself, I think that what went wrong was just being a step-son. What he was resenting, without being aware of it, was not being a "Lord', not being the heir. You see, he wasn't a rebel at all in our sense. That's where Nellie was so silly, always expecting him to join the Communist Party or something idiotic like that.

Martin wasn't that silly, but he was equally silly in his own way. Just as I thought I was making some headway in getting Pugh to see sense, Martin started taking him up and filling his head with all sorts of literary nonsense. He called him his 'Rimbaud manqué' and encouraged just the sort of wild behaviour that Pugh couldn't carry off really at all. What I mean is, that he would always have been rather wild, certainly—that was part of his charm—but it would have been conventional wildness really in, say, the young Guards' Officer tradition. You know what I mean. What he really needed was a conventional framework in which his wildness would be accepted. He was really a very conventional character.

But Martin stuffed him up with all sorts of ideas far above his intellectual station. He was the very opposite of an intellectual. And the result was he became really unbearable, talked an awful lot of nonsense about *actes gratuits* and all sorts of things he didn't understand at all. In effect, all it amounted to was that he became more drunk and silly than ever. He even got himself turned out of the Gargoyle, which was his favourite haunt, and you had to go pretty far to get yourself turned out of the Gargoyle in those days.

So for a month or two I lost connection with him, couldn't get through any more and, of course, it maddened me that it was Martin with all his promises and talk of his new taste for women who was doing it. I think Martin was only experimenting with Judy. And the experiment didn't work. And Pugh showed that it hadn't. Anyhow, luckily Martin went away, you remember, shortly after that, and that was the end of the affair with Pugh, as well.

PUGH'S FILE III

(b)

[*Nellie was too puzzled by the sexual mix-up to make much sense.*]

I simply don't understand what's going on, she said. I really don't. Actually I had been seeing rather more than usual of Martin at the time. He introduced me to Judy who was quite a delightful girl, though politically very uneducated. I found that rather extraordinary. She was a very clever girl, of course, but interested in literature to the exclusion of almost everything. Of course she was working very hard for her degree and had to be single-minded about that. She had her own way to make in the world, and she meant to do it. I admired that.

Yes, they were tremendously fond of each other, I should have said. Why did it all break up? I never got the truth out of anyone. I had several long talks with Judy and I certainly got the impression that marriage was very much in her mind. And Martin was so proud of her. She was very attractive. He'd show her off and loved doing that, and that's where I came in, I think. I took them both round to the Boltons for one of Mother's luncheons, and they made a very good impression, especially her—Judy, I mean. As usual, Mother was at her most exasperating with atrocity stories from Spain, and Judy edged her away from that and

137

got her talking about Yeats whom Mother knew at one time.

I should have thought it was a most successful love affair, and I did get a little cross with Harry at the time. Because Harry talked against it quite violently. I reminded him that back in Dubrovnik he had behaved so sensibly over Elvira. Why couldn't he be equally sensible now over this? He said it was quite different. That Elvira had been a sophisticated woman and knew the score; whereas Judy was very innocent and Martin was leading her up the garden path. That he didn't really love her, was only experimenting, and that it wasn't fair on the girl.

Of course, if that was true, Harry was right to be indignant, and it does rather look now as if he was right, doesn't it? But I didn't think so at the time. I thought that Harry was being very selfish about it, and I told him so.

Actually Harry had come to me soon after it started and asked me to talk seriously to Judy. Was she aware what his—Harry's I mean—position had really been? He said he himself was being excluded more and more from Martin's life and so he couldn't do it himself, though if he got the chance he certainly would. I didn't think that it was really up to me to interfere and, anyhow, from what I saw, they were perfectly happy together. Then when the rift began, Harry darkly hinted that Pugh was in some way responsible. Well, I did tackle Pugh about that. He quite admitted that he found Judy very attractive, and of course they were much the same age. On the other hand they had nothing in common, had they? Her talk about literature would only have bored Pugh, I'm afraid. I can't say I wouldn't have rather encouraged Pugh to see something of her because Pugh was so rootless and drifting at the time. And if he had found Judy attractive enough, perhaps she would have been able to infect him with some of her seriousness. So I wouldn't have been sorry—except from Martin's point of view—if they *had* been seeing a lot of each other.

But, in fact, I'm sure that this didn't happen, and Harry's idea that Pugh had anything to do with them breaking up was, I think, sheer invention. The last talk I had with Judy I brought up the subject of Pugh but she didn't, by then, seem even to like him very much. I was rather hurt at the time; she dismissed him as merely 'an attractive body'. Which wasn't really very like her I thought.

So I don't know what to make of it. It began so promisingly. I really wondered whether Martin wasn't going to settle down, and my own view was that it might be the very best thing for him. And obviously after a bit when her exams were over, Judy would have begun to take more interest in politics. I talked to her about it, of course, from time to time, and though she wasn't reactionary or anything like that, she wasn't also really interested. But that would have come.

No, I don't know where it all went wrong. Perhaps Martin was a little too old and established in his own right for her. She told me she was very flattered by being introduced to everyone in London, but found the famous rather frightening. But I dare say the truth is Harry was right. Martin wasn't as serious as he seemed. He was only experimenting; and then he found this rather unsophisticated Oxford girl a bit below his intellectual station and dropped her. That's, I suppose, what really happened. Something like that. Anyhow, Martin himself didn't want to talk about it afterwards. He obviously blamed himself over it, judging from the few things he did say. For instance he remarked one day, 'When you find you're only using people, you must really stop it, mustn't you?' And in the context this clearly referred to Judy.

(c)

[*Harry makes no bones about his contribution to the affair.*]

I always knew that Martin didn't really want women, he just wanted to know if he could, and I didn't think it at all fair to be leading this poor Judy up the garden. I mean it was all right with Elvira—she was an experienced person and knew her way around and had gone into it with her eyes open. I mean I was there all the time, wasn't I? But Judy was pretty innocent. I'm not sure she even knew what I had been to Martin. She was a very nice girl, more like a boy really, which was half the attraction, if you ask me. But he hadn't any right to lead her on, if he wasn't serious, had he? I mean it was easy for him, wasn't it, being who he is and what he is, to turn the girl's head?

And the same with her. Her stock rose like anything in catching him. I don't say that was the whole of it, but it was quite a big part, I'm sure. And the same with him, because she was one of the most sought-after girls up there then. There aren't many girls available for the boys up there anyhow, and very, very few as attractive as Judy was. So you can imagine it was the talk of the place when they started going round together. He went up there more than ever, and she spent a weekend or two at his flat. Then when term finished, she came to live with him, and he rather cut us all off. It was only natural, I suppose. He didn't want her to see too closely the life he had been living. Anyhow he was very distant if I went round, I know that. I wasn't going to be pushed right out. But he made it as uncomfortable for me as he could. Whenever I arrived, they were just going out, or they'd talk about literature and things that I couldn't keep up with.

She tried to be friendly, and we had two or three cosy gossips when I found her alone sometimes. I tried to warn her, in an indirect way not to expect too much. But she really was in love with him, that was obvious. How much he was with her, I'm not so sure. He was flattered by her devotion and rather proud of himself in carrying her off under the noses of all the boys of her own age. That's what Gavin thinks, and I agree. Well, she stayed there about a month before she had to go back to Oxford. And when she'd gone, we were sort of allowed in again, if you see what I mean, and I thought I'd test out just what it all meant by taking Pugh with me a lot. Of course Martin had met Pugh with me and all of us, but Pugh hadn't made much of an impression. At least, not outwardly, but I thought he probably had, more than appeared. I know the signs, you see. Anyhow Pugh was very discontented at this time. He didn't really know what to do. He was drinking a lot and messing about and complaining that life was so dull.

I suggested to Martin that he might help Pugh to straighten himself out. Martin always responds to an appeal like that, you see, and was prepared to devote hours to anyone's problems, especially if they were as attractive as Pugh was. He always, too, had this special view of people, all his own; and he came to think of Pugh as a sort of Rimbaud, he said, a Rimbaud manqué. And you can imagine how a Rimbaud, even a non-writing Rimbaud, appealed to a Martin. He never got anywhere near suggesting anything that Pugh could do, except the Air Force, which was a good idea really and would have suited Pugh down to the ground in fact. But he wouldn't do that, because it was just the sort of thing his step-father would have admired him for and approved of. So that fell through. And Martin also had what I thought was rather a mad idea that he ought to lose his identity and get a job as a labourer on a building site, or as a petrol pump attendant or something like that. Which only show how impractical Martin really was, for how could you get that sort of job with two million unemployed? Anyhow Pugh didn't a bit want to lose his identity, he wanted to be who he was—he just wanted it to work.

Anyhow, the point was that Martin was soon prepared to spend hours talking to Pugh about his case. I took care to leave them alone a good deal, and when Judy came back unexpectedly one weekend she found them together in bed, I think.

'But do you know that for a fact?'

Well, not exactly. But she obviously did, for she and Martin didn't last a month after that.

No, I didn't feel at all guilty about it. Why should I have done? As I said, I always thought it was unfair of Martin to lead her on if he wasn't serious, and how could he be serious if he really liked boys? And I know he did. And knowing Pugh as I did, I knew that affair wouldn't last, and it didn't either. Pugh just wasn't capable at this time of having a real affair. Look how short a time he lasted with Gavin! Of course he was tremendously flattered, too, by Martin's attentions and by his taking so much trouble over him. But it was all talk, wasn't it?

PUGH'S FILE III

(d)

[Note of a conversation with Martin on the subject.]

One oughtn't to use people, Martin said, and yet I suppose all of us do. And I'm probably unjust to myself in thinking that I used Judy more than she used me. Perhaps we see things in too slick terms nowadays, but it's certainly true that from me she wanted something more like a father's protection than a lover's. Her father died when she was very young. She chose to admire me which is not perhaps the best basis for an affair; for what that really means, doesn't it, is that she idealised me. She expected me to live up to what she wanted from an older man she admired. And, of course, the only consequence could be that the affair for her was a progressive disillusion the more she got to know me. I never came up to the idealisation, and indeed it proved to be just a successive series of let-downs.

But I equally used her. I wanted to prove to myself that my affair with Elvira was not, on similar lines, merely the search for a mother-figure, that I could equally find a young girl attractive enough to go to bed with. I certainly assured myself on that point so that the experiment from my point of view was an unqualified success.

But all it really did for me was to confirm that my real feelings in this direction are for Elvira. And as soon as I realised that, I realised, too, that I had simply been using Judy. Still, I'm not going to blame myself too much. I'm sure the affair didn't damage her. It might even have been healthily disillusioning for her by showing her that the pursuit of a father-figure was a kind of false accident in her development, and that in a proper husband she will find both lover and father.

[*It seemed rather ingenuous of Martin not to have mentioned Pugh as a cause of the break-up. And I wasn't certain he would take it very well if I introduced the subject. But as usual on occasions when he was caught out being less than truthful, he gave the characteristic giggle and admitted that it had something to do with it.*]

But less perhaps than one might think, he said. Harry's story about finding us in bed was pure wish-fulfilment. Pugh certainly had an animal attraction. But as it turned out, this was a wholly surface quality, the immense magnetism of a body, nothing more at all. And with someone so

143

violently attractive, it's only natural to imagine depths tha aren't there. I tried to see him as something more romantic or more romantically suited to my taste. I called him my Rimbaud. But that was a lot of nonsense. If I hadn't been blinded by his absurd beauty I would have recommended him—I should have recommended him—to make himself a high-class courtesan or gigolo. He could have been either or both. What he couldn't be was a dull, self-respecting member of the community.

But it's false to suppose that in this day and age the arrival of a Pugh could come between people like Judy and me. We were too civilised for that. For a moment she did think that perhaps I was having an affair with him, and to be honest, for a time I was, but a romantic affair not a physical one as Harry likes to believe. And short-lived at that. I'd already seen right through Pugh—or rather, I mean, right through my own romanticising of Pugh. Pugh was not to be blamed for being what he was. I was, for wanting to convince my-self that he was really something else. I suppose it is true to say that his being around made her and me look at our re-lationship more objectively and clearly. In that sense you might say he was responsible for us breaking up. But not in the vulgar sense that Harry, I wouldn't be surprised, had hoped for. It didn't turn me back towards Harry. It turned me back to Elvira.

Like many other people, Lady Nellie throughout this period had many a *crise* of conscience about whether or not she should join the Party. Joining a party seems to us now a not particularly important decision. But joining the Communist Party was something different. It was the spiritual equivalent of changing one's religion. It was an act of Faith. The Party, like the Catholics, demanded absolute obedience. If you joined the Party, you had to renounce the freedom of thinking for yourself. You thought what you were told to think. The Party, like the Pope, was infallible. So it was an Act of Renunciation as well as an Act of Faith, and in return for what you gave up, you received Absolute Certainty; and in this critical time, when most people were worried sick by not knowing what to believe about a world running dangerously down hill, certainty was a great comfort. By joining one put oneself in other people's hands, people who claimed to KNOW. Or, to put it more in their terms, one allied oneself with History.

But it was always an agonising decision, and Nellie, like Martin, had duly agonised over it before, unlike him, finally committing herself:

PUGH'S FILE IV

(a)

[*Gavin professed the smallest possible interest in whether or not Nellie joined the Party.*]

Who cares in the slightest one way or another, he said. All this fuss and talk going on day after day about whether a silly woman does or doesn't do a silly thing that won't make the slightest difference to the world one way or the other. Martin holding conferences late into the night. Harry, at his most pompous, and Nellie dithering to and fro as if the future of the Spanish War depended on her decision. It's all too absurd.

Anyhow, I can tell you she will. It's just the sort of thing ex-Catholics like her do. They need some religion with really fixed principles and, having lost her own, she's on the look out for a new set. I've always said she was a silly woman and doesn't really understand what she's talking about. What people like that want is a Faith and that's what she'll get with the Party. Martin doesn't want her to because, if she does, the whole question of whether he should, becomes more urgent. And it's really the last thing he wants to do. He values his ability to flirt with every party much too much. Of course, he's being wooed by the Communists. He really would be rather a catch. But he's being wooed by everyone else as well, and that suits him down to the ground. Nellie isn't being wooed by anyone. Who would want her except for her title? That's all the Communists want. She'll be a seven-day propaganda point, and then they'll find out what an ass she is and keep her out of the papers and out of harm's way.

Of course, Harry's trying to persuade her. Partly to

ustify his being a Party member himself, partly because she'd be rather a catch for him. Actually, you know, Harry's been in rather bad odour with the Party, for all his talk. Not unnaturally, for after the first enthusiastic month when the Spanish thing began, he started to become a very slack member again. As I knew he would. Which was Harry always going to prefer, a night out with Pugh at the Gargoyle or an evening distributing pamphlets with the Comrades? It stands to reason. Harry was never meant for all that puritan nonsense. He practically never attends Cell meetings now, and if they were so strict as they used to be, I should think they would expel him or ex-communicate him, or whatever it is they do.

So if he could go along with *Lady* Nellie in tow, it would do him some good, and I really believe that's the only interest he has in it. What Nellie's indecision has done, actually, is to revive his enthusiasm temporarily which makes him very boring just as he was beginning to be fun again.

I wish Nellie would join and get it over with. I'm certain she's going to sooner or later. This prolonged religious crisis of hers is a great trial. Why, it's even affecting Pugh, who hardly really knows what the Party is and is bored to death when Nellie tries to explain. But he half thinks it would be rather fun if she did, just because it would shake his step-father. Though, personally, I don't think it would even do that. He must know how dotty she is already and be prepared for anything.

Actually Pugh gets a certain amount of amusement out of it, because he goes round to his Grandmother who also adores him and plays them off one against the other. The Old Lady really would be hurt if Nellie actually joined the Party and uses Pugh partly as a spy, so to speak, and partly as a persuader. She told him that if he could stop Nellie joining, she'd seriously consider helping him to go to America, which is what he really wants. On the other hand, you see, the very fact that it would upset her mother is a strong reason for Nellie to join. Probably much stronger than any ideological motive, if the truth were known.

Anyhow, Pugh trots between the two stirring up trouble in a very mischievous way—there's no malice in him—just for the fun of hearing them inveighing against each other. And as he draws his allowance from Nellie and gets a fiver out of the Old Lady every time he goes round, he's doing pretty well out of it.

Why is Nellie so undecided? It's a weapon she is using against her family. As long as she keeps the threat over them, she thinks she's upsetting them. She may talk about it in terms of ideology—is the Popular Front more important than the Party and all that? But it's just a family wrangle. She used it against her husband, too, but he refused to be intimidated. Now he's dead, there's really nothing to stop her. But on the other hand the very fact that he's not there to forbid it makes the prospect less attractive. It no longer seems such a great liberating act of defiance, as it was then.

Actually Pugh is one reason why she doesn't at the moment, I think. He doesn't really want his aunt getting into the papers as a Communist. That's not at all his idea of what his family should be like. Because he never forgets the sort of background he really belongs to, and wants to belong to.

And she thinks the world of Pugh; she really loves him and spends a lot of time worrying about him and wishing she could find something to settle him down, the trouble being that reconciling him with his family and his background—which is the one thing that *would* settle him down— is just the one thing she can't bring herself to do. So she gives him this allowance, which is enough to prevent him from settling down to anything, and then complains that he doesn't! So like her!

But if Pugh went away or something like that, disappeared in some way from our circle, then I think she'd find herself ready for it. But as I say, what on earth does it matter one way or the other? Nellie doesn't matter tuppence.

PUGH'S FILE IV

(b)

[Nellie explained herself like this.]

Of course I had long been considering joining the Party, ever since Jonathan's days. I was pretty well convinced from early on when I first became a Socialist that the only hope for real Socialism lay in Communism. The whole Labour Party doctrine of the 'inevitability of gradualness' always struck me as mere idealism. The more one read Marx and Lenin, the more surely one saw where that sort of compromise led one. And then the history of the Labour Party in the last few years reinforced that view.

It wasn't only that by joining the National Government Ramsay Macdonald had smashed the Labour Party for many years to come; it was also that the Labour rump, by its hesitations over Hitlerism, and indeed over everything else, showed that it didn't really mean business. I mean, if we're going to have a worker's Britain with the means of production in the worker's control, it's no use compromising, is it? It's something that has to be fought for full out. You can't compromise with Capitalism, can you? Once you start that you'll find they're much too clever for you, for one thing!

And then there was always the example of the USSR for us to draw on. There you really have a Worker's State with all that that implies.

Well, you know all that; I needn't go into it. Every argument of logic and reason leads me to Communism. And so the Party is the only logical thing to join. I hesitated for two reasons really. The first was that I felt rather silly being Lady Esmeralda and joining the Worker's Party. You see what I mean. I didn't think they'd ever really accept me. That's why I wanted to drop my title. But, of course, Jonathan wouldn't hear of it, any more than he'd hear of me joining the Party. That was the second reason why I couldn't. I often threatened to. We had terrible rows over it. But I saw that it hurt him really too much. I suppose one shouldn't be put off by things like that. As Harry often says, 'This is the final crisis, and people are bound to be hurt.'

But I couldn't really persuade myself that my joining would make all that difference—to them, I mean. And if it was going to hurt Jonathan that much, well, I couldn't somehow do it.

When Jonathan died and I was free to do as I liked, then, somehow, I don't quite know why, it didn't seem so urgent. I think this was partly because by this time I had great hope of the Popular Front. The French *Front Populaire* seemed to me a terrific step forward and I became convinced that we needed the same thing here. After all it's no use denying what Martin says that the CP is only really a tiny task force. On its own it isn't big enough or powerful enough to have any real effect, is it? It would be years and years before it could be in a position to seize power. It's true Lenin's Party started as a tiny group who miraculously did convert the whole of Russia. But they were in a bigger crisis even than we are, a war crisis, which we aren't yet. Perhaps when we are, in a year or two, the CP's chance will come. But meanwhile what had become urgent was to get the Government out and reverse their policy *vis-à-vis* the dictators, and surely the best chance of doing that was the Popular Front?

Harry used to argue that the Party were really the leading element in the Popular Front, the whole spine and guts of
150

it, and I think that is true. They really are dedicated in a way that nobody else quite is. I used to go round with him to his Cell sometimes—he was trying his best to persuade me to join. And it was very impressive, no doubt about it.

I loved the atmosphere. There was the small library of the Party literature, Marx, Engels, Lenin, Palme Dutt, and all the orange volumes of the Left Book Club: the Soviet posters on the walls, and later that great map of Spain with its pegs to mark the battle positions. Against the walls, the banners that would be carried in processions. On the tables, all the pamphlets they were to distribute, the leaflets and the *Daily Workers*. And they were all very serious and hard-working. There was so much to be done, door-to-door calls to be made, recruits to be got, study-circles to be formed, marches and demonstrations to be attended. It was a real hive of political activity, a Party Cell, unlike anything else you saw anywhere. I was very attracted.

But then came the usual snag. They were very attentive to me always, plied me with cups of tea, and sprinkled my title in every phrase of their conversation. Lady Nellie this and Lady Nellie that. I begged them not to, and they were genuinely shocked.

'But it's a great asset, Lady Nellie,' the serious, prim little secretary explained. 'You mustn't be ashamed of it. People at large think the Party only consists of the working masses. But that's not so. All classes are members of the Party now; we're all Honorary Members of the Proletariat. But just because there are still people—middle-class people—frightened of the movement because they think it's only a working-class movement, the more they hear of people like you joining, the better it is for us.'

Still I didn't like it. They seemed to want me more for my title than anything else.

So, though I was very impressed always by their dedication and devotion and though I knew that all logic was on their side, I didn't feel right about it. I didn't want to go on always being *Lady* Nellie! It's all very well calling us Honorary Members of the Proletariat, but how can you feel that when you're *Lady* Nellie all the time? I wanted just to merge with them and be one of them. But they wouldn't have that. Harry said I oughtn't to mind. We all had to bring to the Party whatever gifts we had, and my title was one of mine. But it was all very well for him. He really is a member of the Proletariat, a real working-class boy. There's no difficulty for him. He wouldn't see how different it was for me.

Anyhow, as I say, the Popular Front did seem to me the great solution of everything, and more than ever when the Spanish War started, and they formed their Popular Front. If only there was a Popular Front in England, as now in France and in Spain, surely the three of us could unite with the USSR and win this battle? And I was reinforced in this view when I remembered Martin's Elvira and how she and her friends fought Fascism without being Communists.

Still, I'm not saying I didn't feel guilty about not joining, because I did, when all I really believed in and all I read seemed to point that way. But there was another reason for hesitating now. Pugh's arrival in London was a great anxiety to me. I did so want him to find his feet and interest himself in all the things that were going on and were so important, and I did so hope that by being with Harry and seeing all of us so busy with it all, that he would. Naturally I didn't expect it at once.

He first of all had to get over the experience of that appalling school David had sent him to. And then you see he couldn't have helped having absorbed a thoroughly reactionary outlook in his home background. When I talked to him about it, it was obvious that the very word 'Communist' was something he thought of as beyond the pale. I thought I might be able to influence him a bit towards being less Tory than he was—and I think I did. But if I mentioned Communism or Russia he shied away at once. One has to be very careful with boys from his kind of background. So I took care to talk only in the most general terms. And I thought—in fact I still think—that I was making some headway with him. I knew it was going to be a slow process. But I knew, too, that if I were actually a Communist, if I actually joined the Party, I should lose all influence with him at once.

I'm sure I was right about that. And you know as well as I do how badly poor Pugh needed a good influence at the time. He didn't seem to be able to settle to anything. He was just frittering his time away: and I did hear rumours of his behaving very badly at that Gargoyle place. Well, of course, he was very young and the freedom he had rather went to his head.

But then came the really shocking thing of his trying to join the Carlists and all that. You can imagine what that did to me. What was the good of my trying to teach him the elements of Socialism, if he could do a thing like that? Obviously, I said to myself—in anger, I suppose—I've had no influence on him at all. And then that wretched David backing him up over it and positively approving until he found it threatened his position! It all thoroughly upset me and so I took my decision. I'd show them both. I'd join the Party and I did.

They put it in headlines in the *Daily Worker*, of course, and the other papers got on to me, and it was all there too—'Earl's daughter goes Red!', 'Under-Secretary's sister joins the Duchess!' and all that.

Actually Pugh's reaction was only to laugh. He didn't seem a bit upset after all. He took the penny papers round to the Boltons where they have only *The Times* and *Telegraph*, and their reaction was awfully flat. David just said, 'Fancy her falling for that lot!' and Mother raised her eyes to Heaven and said 'Le Bon Dieu forgive her.' But it was a three-days' wonder, that was all.

To be absolutely honest, it was rather disappointing for me, too. I was buttered up at the first Cell meeting, but the Secretary told me that probably what would be wanted of me now was some public speaking, and above all, appearances on various platforms, and that would be arranged by Party Headquarters. And not very much has come of that. I've appeared on the platform three or four times, and this, you see, simply drives me further away from the real workers. As I thought, they're just using my title for its publicity value. Just what I didn't want. So mostly I see that I shall just be sitting on platforms like a dummy, lending my name to the proceedings. Harry says it's all valuable. But it doesn't feel very valuable to me.

I am quite certain in my own mind that it was Pugh who was primarily responsible for the misappropriation of Nellie's £700. Harry acquiesced in it, of course, and thoroughly enjoyed the spending of it, but without Pugh's prompting I very much doubt if he would have had the audacity to do it himself.

It was difficult to get at the truth of this incident. As will be seen, Harry prevaricated, and a slightly false version was given Nellie to spare her feelings both for Harry and for Pugh. But what came out in the end was simply this: the money was put up by Nellie to help a Jewish refugee girl escape from Germany. Harry was to handle the deal, but Pugh and he, finding themselves with £700 in fivers, used it for themselves. Harry told Nellie—or at least implied to her—that the 'contact' to whom he had given the money had gone off with it without fulfiling his part of the bargain, a risk—he implied—they always had to take. But when Martin, who had been away in Vienna, returned, he met the 'contact' and discovered the truth, namely that Harry had simply never turned up for the appointment at which the money should have been handed over.

When Harry gave me his version he was obviously putting the best face on it he could in the circumstances:

PUGH'S FILE V

(a)

Pugh was wilder than ever after coming back from Gavin's, Harry told me, up to every mischief and throwing himself into any fun that came along. And as I was upset just about then over Martin, we had some mad times together.

'What sort of mad times?'

Oh, nothing out of the way: the usual things. There was this night club, the Gargoyle. You remember it, with mirrors all round the walls and a mirrored floor? There was a bar downstairs, and dancing and dinner upstairs. We used to go there very often. There were some nice people around, too. And when Pugh was sober, which wasn't very often, he used to end up in anyone's bed who wanted him, and most people did. When he was drunk, he usually ended up in mine. Just a romp, you understand. I liked Pugh very well, but it wasn't an affair or anything. He did have that affair with Gavin. At least I presume so. But as I've said, they were very secretive about it, which wasn't like Gavin at all. He usually told everything.

I don't know what happened. Pugh wouldn't say anything. And he was worse than ever just after that week. They finally turned him out of the Gargoyle. He got so drunk, pawed everyone, and generally made a nuisance of himself. And he got badly into debt there, too. I couldn't afford all those dinners and drinks we had. So he had to pay for them.

And so all that money business, and this really did get us both into trouble. As you know, Nellie often supplied money to get refugees out of Germany; and Martin had a particularly difficult case at the time, that I was trying to help with. She was a German Jewish girl, a painter, and nearly all the arrangements were made. I was to marry her as soon as she got here, to give her English citizenship. You see, it didn't matter to me marrying her. Quite a lot of us were volunteering to do this at the time. We could get a divorce after, easy. But it needed about £700 to get this girl out. Now, in the middle of the negotiations, they seemed to run up against some snag we couldn't get over, and the whole thing seemed to be off, so Martin went off to Vienna to see Elvira. Then, suddenly the snags came clear, and our contact was ready for the money.

I couldn't get hold of Martin, so I appealed to Nellie. And she provided the money. It had to be in cash, and she handed it to me in her house, all in fivers. I went home with it. Then an unfortunate thing happened. I couldn't get hold of the contact that night, and meanwhile in came Pugh, and there was I sitting with £700 in fivers.

Now, Pugh had been desperate to get back in again with the Gargoyle, and the secretary had told him that when he paid up his debts, perhaps they would let him in again. And that was £25 or so. So he suggested the next day we go to the races, win the £25, and we'd be quids in. He had an infallible system, he said. I suppose we got a bit tight and I let him talk me into it. I don't say it was all his fault. But I did have second thoughts the next morning, but Pugh wouldn't listen. He said he'd take full responsibility for getting it back somehow if anything went wrong, which it wouldn't. So I agreed.

Pugh's system wasn't infallible, and when we came away, we were £75 shy. This was so much it didn't seem worth not going to the Gargoyle and settling that up; and so, on the following morning, we were short by just over a hundred. The contact eventually rang me, and I tried to bluff it out with £600. But he wouldn't have it, and finally said unless I could bring the whole seven within an hour, the deal would be off. Well, Pugh couldn't get a hundred in an hour, where could he? I couldn't go back to Nellie. So we were left with £600. I couldn't return it a hundred short to Nellie. I just stalled with her, implying that the contact hadn't let me know anything yet. Then, when Martin came back a week later, I bluffed it out: I just told him that this particular scheme had failed. So Pugh and I had six hundred to spend.

'What did you do with it?'

It's amazing how quick six hundred can go, if you're living it up a bit, isn't it? We went to all the posh restaurants and ended up most nights at the Café de Paris or on from there to the Gargoyle. Then there was Pugh's system on the horses—because we hoped to get back our losses still that way, and put ourselves in the clear. But it didn't work, and by the time we'd wasted a couple of hundred on that, it wasn't difficult to get rid of the rest. We had some fun though, while it lasted.

'Didn't you realise you were bound to be found out sooner or later?'

I don't think so. I didn't think Nellie would miss £700. But that's the worst of the very rich, isn't it? They do notice. They hand you out a great wodge of money as if it meant nothing to them. But they haven't forgotten at all. Even so I reckoned that by the time Martin came back it would all have passed over, and in any case it was quite likely that Martin and Nellie wouldn't meet because Martin was all over the place lecturing at the time. So it was just bad luck that they did happen to, and Nellie did happen to say that she'd like to meet the girl who was saved, and when were we going to get married, and could she be there? So it all came out.

'And what happened then?'

You can imagine the row. I suppose Martin had to pay Nellie back. I don't know what arrangement they came to. But I do know we were very unpopular for a bit.

'Not surprisingly!'

I suppose not. On the other hand I didn't feel too bad about it as far as Martin was concerned, though I didn't like having done that to Nellie. But Martin wasn't exactly generous to me, you know. I guess I was owed a good time and we had it!

'And what about the refugee?'

I expected they'd find some other way of getting her out, now they knew. But I'll tell you what it really did to me: it made me fed up with the whole thing, with Martin and England and everything else!

PUGH'S FILE V

(b)

[*Nellie gave me her account of this affair.*]

Nothing that's happened has so upset me as this. It isn't the money, that isn't the point. As a matter of fact, when Jonathan died he left me quite a sum, much more than I'd expected, and this was just the kind of thing I wanted to use it on.

Martin and I had combined several times before in these operations, so, you see, it didn't seem to me at all surprising when Harry came round in a great state, because they were asking for the money to get out this Jewish girl—the one he was going to marry—and Martin was away—which I knew he was—and Harry had to have the money at once. He was worried about the whole thing because normally it was Martin who made the actual arrangements. And to me the arrangement seemed rather amateur. Harry was to meet this man at the Café Royal. He was to sit down at a certain table reading the Londoner's Diary in the *Evening Standard*. And then this man who he didn't know would sit down next to him and open a conversation about the last paragraph but one. That's how he'd know he was genuine: and then he, Harry I mean, was to hand over the £700 in fivers.

All that seemed convincing enough, but what I didn't understand was how we were able to be sure that this man would keep his side of the bargain. But Harry assured me it was always done like this. One has to trust them, and hadn't every one we'd tried so far been all right?

And that was quite true. So after some discussion we went along to the bank, and I cashed my cheque, and gave the money to Harry. He was to let me know that it had gone off all right by telephoning that evening, which he did. But he seemed a bit worried and in the end told me he was doubtful if he ought to have parted with the money. There was something suspicious about that contact. Still, he had finally decided to go ahead.

Now I'm quite certain in my own mind that this wasn't just a plan for getting money out of me, as Gavin has been saying. I'm sure it wasn't. I'm sure that something or other went wrong. When I did see Harry, he told me again that he had met the man as arranged with all that *Evening Standard* business. It had all gone well, but he, Harry that is, hadn't much liked the look of the fellow. But what could he do? He had to trust him and the man had said that he would be getting in touch as soon as transport was arranged for the girl, but that nothing had happened so far. He'd let me know as soon as anything did.

I was away for a week or two after that, and I didn't think much about it. But I happened to be on the platform at a meeting in Birmingham a week or two later when Martin was one of the Speakers, and I asked him if any news had been heard of our refugee girl. Martin said, 'But it's all off for the moment, didn't Harry tell you'?' I said I'd been away and hadn't heard from Harry, and did that mean that the £700 was lost. Martin asked 'What £700?' and I told him about Harry coming to me. 'But I thought Harry told me that the whole deal was called off before any money was handed over,' he said, rather puzzled. 'I must look into this.'

So later that week in London Martin came round to me rather shame-faced and tried to explain what had happened. Harry's contact had never turned up at the Café Royal that night, and Harry had just kept the money, and Pugh and he had spent it. Martin was very indignant about it and insisted on paying it back; but I said as Pugh had probably spent his share we should go halves, which we did.

But, of course, it wasn't so much a question of the money. Still, you see how it shook my faith in Harry. Well, yes, and in Pugh I suppose, too. But I'm sure that Harry was a much stronger personality than Pugh and had led him astray. Besides Pugh never professed any beliefs, did he? Whereas Harry was supposed to be dedicated.

Martin was very ashamed for Harry, but it wasn't his fault, Martin's I mean, after all. All I felt was I didn't want to see Harry again for some time—or Pugh.

I actually had a long letter from Harry, not excusing himself, but trying to explain and, of course, I do see that it's very tempting for someone who's never had money suddenly to be landed with £700. It's a great temptation, and Martin was deliberately keeping him very short at this time. I'm not sure that was wise. What Harry explained was that the contact had never turned up at the Café Royal, and Pugh had come in and found him with all that money and persuaded him to go out on the town, and then next day had suggested winning back what they'd spent at the races, and that hadn't worked. So that they were £100

F

short and couldn't face me. So they tried the races again and gradually it went.

Well, I see how that kind of thing happens (though I didn't like Harry putting all the blame on Pugh). Anyhow I'm not going to quarrel over money. It's no good pretending it doesn't make a difference, because it does. But I forgave them both.

Martin was even more horrified than me. In fact he was very unforgiving. I think wrongly, myself. After all we both have had money and they never have, and no harm was really done in the end. I think that Martin's unforgiving attitude really caused all that followed.

Author's Note

What Martin found it hard to forgive was that, in fact, Harry hadn't just failed to meet the contact as he had told Nellie. The truth was that the contact had telephoned while Martin was away. Harry had answered the call and—at this stage with the best of intentions—agreed to meet the contact two days on in order to give himself time to get the money together. He decided it was no use trying to wire Martin— the contact had already demurred at the delay. So he got it from Nellie. But then when Pugh and he found themselves with £700 in cash in their pockets, temptation was too strong. And he simply never kept the appointment. But this contact was, as it happened, a particularly reliable one, who got in touch with Martin the moment he got back, So it all came out:

(c)

I never told Nellie, Martin said, the exact truth. I let her believe the story Harry told her, because if she had known that a real chance of rescuing that poor Jewish girl had been there and been lost by Harry's weakness, she never would have forgiven him. And there didn't seem any point in that. But I knew. And I couldn't forgive him so easily. What frightened me was that, as Gavin had prophesied, Harry's behaviour might be symptomatic of a deeper instability.

My fault? No. I'm quite sure I was right in pushing him off on his own both for his own good and for mine. I know that I, anyhow, have done much better work since he left me. What is worrying is that he still does nothing. I deceived myself into thinking this didn't matter, as he was working so hard for the Party and was so serious about it. But how serious could he possibly be if he lets this wretched girl rot in Germany so that he and Pugh could have fun with the money they'd stolen—and stolen really, when it comes down to it, from her? All it means is that all his talk of Communism is complete nonsense.

'Come now, this wasn't really stealing. They just started something they couldn't stop. And wasn't Pugh the one most to blame anyhow?'

Of course I blame Pugh, but in quite a different way. Pugh would never have cared one way or the other about a refugee. Pugh simply stole his share from his aunt, quite straightforwardly—or from me (with a characteristic giggle) in point of fact. Now if Harry had stolen the money directly or indirectly from me, I should be worried in quite a
164

different way. I should have recognised it as a pretty straightforward blow aimed at my having deserted him. But this is different. This is aimed to make nonsense of his whole life as he's living it at the present, and, even worse, at the whole of the life we lived together. It was a studied and deliberate betrayal of all we had stood for, of everything he'd learned from me.

As I say, I hoped the CP really meant something to him, and that he would find himself some work. I deliberately gave him only a very small allowance, because I wanted him to do that. And I imagined he wouldn't be able to face the other Party members just as a kept boy, and that this would be another inducement for him to find himself something. I didn't think I had yet spoiled him so completely that he would be content to do nothing at all. If I had, that's when I should feel responsible. But one can't go on feeling responsible for ever. People must take *some* responsibility for their own lives, even the Harrys of this world.

I won't be made to feel guilty for having given him so many advantages. And I have. Why pretend? Potentially he's a better person than he was when I picked him up. After all, what was he, then? In effect, a male tart. If I had simply used him and left him as many others did, should I feel guilty or responsible? It would need a sort of Tolstoyan conscience to feel guilty about everyone one had slept with. And if I had just been a casual encounter like the others, where would he have ended up? I've given him the possibility of a life. If he can't take it, is that my fault? I absolutely refuse any guilt over it. I know he'll try to play on it, perhaps all his life. But I must have the strength to refuse to be blackmailed. I've given him the chance. If he throws it away, that's his fault and no one else's.

The weak have no right to ruin other people's lives as well as their own. And it's only weakness to let them. But it isn't easy at all to be strong enough to resist this kind of blackmail. There's a sense in which I love Harry still. But I'm not going to see my love simply draining away into weakness or worse. What he's done this time is the worst thing he's ever done. And he's done a good deal of damage already, you know. I wonder—or have wondered—whether he isn't just one of those destructive people, who, having nothing to make of themselves, want no one else to make anything of themselves either. When we were together, it was painful to watch him frittering his life away. It even came to his resenting my work, as if it was something that divided us.

Perhaps what I have to do now is cut myself off from him completely, throw him absolutely on his own resources and see how that works. What do you think?

'I think the whole business might be disastrous.'

I don't see how or why. And if it were I suppose a rescue operation could be mounted. But I think it has to be tried. It's either that or—what? In any case, I'm not having him back—ever.

Author's Note

What Martin actually did was even more drastic. He didn't cut Harry off, but he did tell him absolutely firmly that he wasn't ever going to live with him again, and very shortly afterwards he publicly announced his engagement to Elvira who had come over to England for a week or two. I don't know whether Martin had calculated how great an effect this would have on Harry. He meant it, I dare say, only as a reinforcement of his warning that they would never be together again. The effect it actually had on Harry was something different, and Harry's reaction to it took Martin, it seemed, completely by surprise. Harry decided to join the International Brigade and fight in Spain.

PART FOUR

Spain

Harry and Gavin had made the decision to join the International Brigade and fight in Spain while Martin was away. As soon as Pugh discovered they had joined, he persuaded them to help him to join, too. So all three were going off together. In order to prevent her stopping him again, the decision was carefully concealed from Nellie, so I have no record of her reactions to the decision. Gavin gave me an account of how it came about:

We decided on it, Harry and I, while Martin was away after announcing his engagement, Gavin told me. Martin went back to Vienna with Elvira for a week, and it was during that time that we fixed it up. We'd met the second night in the Café Bleu which we'd rather taken to lately—there was nice music played there softly at night. Harry had come in from a Cell meeting and was unusually quiet, and when I questioned him, he came out with it. 'What about going to Spain? Have you thought of it?' Well, of course I had, vaguely, for ages. Ever since the fiasco with Pugh.

So I was instantly attracted by Harry's suggestion. I only wondered if they'd have me. After all, Harry had a lot to offer. He was a trained soldier, more, had had what was supposed to be the best training in the world. And then he was a paid up member of the CP who organised the Brigade. But what had I got to offer? Absolutely nothing.

But Harry brushed that aside. Of course they'd want me. They wanted anyone they could get, and I was intelligent, wasn't I? I'd soon learn.

So we talked it over for a couple of days and it seemed, in the dim blue light of the Café Bleu, a romantic sort of adventure. I'm not even sure how seriously we were taking it at that stage. We were day-dreaming about it really, and after a couple of days of that Harry rang up to call it off. I tried to persuade him to go on with it: but he was clearly in a state of dither. What we finally did was postpone a decision.

Meanwhile Martin had come back and one night he telephoned and begged me to come round. He told me that he had just had a flaming row with Harry, and Harry had ended up by flinging out of the door and shouting out, as he left, that he was going to Spain, that we'd talked it over and he'd now decided he would definitely go.

Martin wanted me to persuade Harry out of it; that I wasn't going to do. In fact I had felt it as a terrific let-down when Harry had first cried off.

But now it was evidently on again, and the last thing I was going to do was try and persuade Harry to change his mind if he really meant it now. I imagined he was trying to get hold of me at this very moment (which turned out afterwards to have been the case), and I was itching to get away from Martin and get in touch with him.

But poor Martin was really agonised about it. I felt quite sorry for him. He argued round and round about the absurdity of Harry's decision. But I wouldn't see it as absurd. 'After all, Spain's very important and Harry would be quite good I should think."

'Balls!' said Martin. 'He'll be absolutely hopeless, you know he will. He'll do nothing but grouch and complain. Have you really, either of you, thought what it's going to be like, in reality, in hard fact?'

I don't know that I had, but I wasn't telling Martin so. To me it was a solution. I was more determined than ever on it. I said I thought Harry had really thought it through and everything led there, both his training and his beliefs.

'What beliefs?' said Martin. 'The beliefs he was able to throw over without a thought when it came to living it up with Pugh? How far will those beliefs carry him when he's up against real discomfort and danger? Be your age, Gavin. You know this is romantic nonsense. You could stop him if you wanted and I think you're the only person who could. I know I can't. We've reached a stage where we've no real contact. But you could dissuade him.'

Of course, the thing was I didn't want to. But I did find it rather hard to explain my position to Martin. I find it rather hard to explain it to myself. It just seems a solution. What sort of a solution, and of what, I can't really say.

Martin accused me of being simply suicidal. 'Do you *want* to be killed?'

My answer to that—and it isn't just melodramatics—is that I don't mind. I really don't. I don't think I will be, of course. But it's a risk one can't entirely overlook. I hadn't. I'd faced that. If it was to be that, I just didn't mind. And Martin's arguments against my going—that I was wasting myself and my gifts—seemed to me, in my peculiar context, beside the point. I have gifts, I suppose, yes. But what was I doing with them at the moment?

'It's not even as if you cared all that much,' Martin said.

And that's true, too. At least I do care in a sort of way, sometimes. But anyhow I admit it's not the Cause that's taking me there. I can't believe in those sorts of abstracts. Perhaps it's just to get away from tedious arguments like this one with Martin! Once you're committed, there you are.

Anyhow he saw he wasn't going to get anywhere by arguing over my case and he reverted to Harry again. Surely I could see that Harry was going, if he was going, for some very personal reason? And was that the spirit in which to make such a fateful decision?

I won't say Martin was wrong, but I could tell him that that wasn't how Harry saw it. When we had first talked about it while he (Martin) was away, Harry's arguments were all in terms of thinking it his duty. He was single, independent, free, no ties or family considerations; and then, with his training, wasn't he just the kind of person they were looking for? How could he go on, just doing routine Party work when everything seemed to point to this decision? He felt that all the comrades in his Cell were wondering why he didn't volunteer—he was so obviously the ideal material.

'So he's just trapped by guilt,' Martin said. 'That, again,

is absolutely no good reason for going. The comrades obviously haven't the slightest idea of the kind of person Harry really is—or they'd see at once that he was quite unsuitable.'

But I refused to see it, till at last I escaped and went off in search of Harry, and found him at the Café Bleu. This time his mind was really made up, and we agreed to go round and enrol the very next morning; and in due course, we did.

SPANISH FILE II

[The following extract from Gavin's novel gives a good idea of how things were organised and what joining up felt like.]

Gavin was there first, as usual. He walked patiently up and down the narrow street in front of the little bookshop above which were the committee rooms. He was too familiar with the books displayed—in their startlingly yellow jackets, their portraits of the familiar faces, Marx, Engels, Lenin —for them to attract his attention from his own nervous nausea; that cold feeling in the belly which preceded any frightening event, a football game on a cold wet day, or an interview with the dentist. He paused to look at them for a moment, and then, because they didn't hold him, passed on. He looked at his watch. Why was Harry always late?

He stopped at the café two doors down—a workers' café. An urn was steaming behind the rough counter. On oil-clothed tables thick steaming mugs were standing. On the wall hung a notice, 'Coffee, tuppence a cup'. He half moved to go in, then hesitated as if it were some exclusive club to which he, being only a newly elected member, hadn't quite the courage to assert his right of entry.

He turned back and walked past the shop again, looked at his watch, scanned the corner expecting to see Harry turning it. His sickness was worse; it was mounting.

He went past the bookshop to the corner and looked down the street. Still no sign of Harry. Deliberately he lit a cigarette. He looked in the window of the shop, a second-hand store. There was a pile of suitcases and haversacks. Should he have a rucksack? There were a number of knives. A knife surely was essential? He imagined himself with a hunk of bread and a sausage; taking out a clasp-knife, cutting

174

the sausage in rounds, eating it from the point of the knife. Up beyond was a balaclava helmet, with warm ear-pieces. They said Madrid was horribly cold. He always felt it in his ears. He had vague memories of runs at school on dull December afternoons in bitter winds. The relief of getting back to a warm shower—if the water was warm, which it often wasn't. This was going to be like an afternoon run prolonged for months. He could feel the sensation of freezing, stinging on the edges of his ears.

He looked at his watch: stamped his feet to get warmth into them. Harry was always late.

There was a flask with a leather case, such as is used for hunting. He might have that filled with brandy. There would be *that* difference. It wasn't quite like going to school again. A torch would be useful, too. But perhaps not allowed there, either: not to prevent reading after dark (a beatable offence), but it might guide bombers. Bombers. A quaking, shattering reverberation: the screams of the wounded; his own perhaps. He put the thought aside.

The window was full of useful gadgets, a knife-fork-and-spoon, a tiny spirit stove, a compass, a pair of binoculars. They began to assume a new reality, things he would have dismissed or passed by as 'camping-gear', with associations of Boy Scouts. They were suddenly of immensely serious importance: things which might make all the difference.

'Hello, Gavin. I'm afraid I'm a bit late.'

Harry had come up behind him, smiling confidently. 'Let's go in shall we?'

As they approached the bookshop once more, Gavin became overwhelmed with a sense of his own incompetence. Harry had been in the Guards so that he was experienced and proficient. While Gavin had refused to join the school OTC on pacifist grounds. It had been one of his longest struggles with his housemaster, Mr Selwyn—an ex-officer. Night after night for three weeks of one term,

Mr Selwyn had badgered him; but he had obstinately refused. He had, at least partly, been buoyed up by a sense of being politically a martyr; instead apparently he was, politically, a fool.

They went through the bookshop into a narrow passage. A number of other people, all workers, seeming to Gavin all much tougher and more efficient than he could ever be, stood along the passage. They pushed their way through and went into a low-ceilinged untidy room behind. Someone was speaking at the telephone: 'But tonight's the Shoreditch meeting. I've got to get there.'

There were two or three typewriters, an air of slightly bungled efficiency. A woman of perhaps thirty-five, small, harassed, untidy, greeted them: her tone was injured as if their visit was an intrusion on her time.

'What do *you* want, Comrades?'

Harry answered with some elation in his voice: 'We want to go to Spain.'

But the announcement did not have the effect which Gavin had expected; the very opposite.

'Well, you aren't the only ones. There are lots of other Comrades here before you. Take your turn in the queue—outside in the passage.'

Disconcerted, they went outside and took their place behind the others. There wasn't very long to wait. In a moment or two they were called back into the big room.

'Anyone got an appointment?' the woman asked. There was no answer. 'Well, it's no good your coming without appointments. We're all too busy. You'll all have to make appointments. Meanwhile you can fill in these forms.'

She was brisk and off-hand, where Gavin had expected something dramatic; he felt as if he had been justly rebuked. He took a form and went over with Harry to fill it up.

Question one: name. He filled that up. *Question two: are you a member of the Party? What branch?* He left a blank. *Question three: if not, what working-class organisation do you belong to?* He left another blank. *Question four: recommended by.......................... who is a member of.............*

He turned to Harry, embarrassed by having nothing to put down.

'Shall I say recommended by you, Harry?'

But Harry wasn't there any longer. Three other people had come in, all tall, tough, working-class. The leading one, Bill, was huge with a chest like a stove.

'Bill! What are you doing here? You coming too?' Harry and he were shaking hands, clapping shoulders, being introduced to the others. Perfunctorily Harry introduced Gavin. They were men he had known in the Guards.

'We must stick together,' Harry was saying. 'Christ, this is marvellous; we'll make up a machine-gun section.' He was very excited at having two people with him whose qualities as soldiers he knew. Gavin felt shut out from them. He would be more of a drag than a help. These were Harry's own kind and shared the relevant experience. He returned, punctured and inferior, to his form.

Question five: what military training have you had? Give particulars of certificates, etc. He looked blankly at this and wondered if he should write down something. Four years in the OTC perhaps? Why not? He turned to ask Harry, but Harry was exchanging reminiscences with his new friends. He saw that on Harry's sheet everything was filled up. The name of his branch followed by an imposing array of military accomplishments. Gavin turned to the next question.

Question six: reasons for wanting to go to Spain. There must be some formula which covered it. He couldn't go into the whole of that. He wrote down, Anti-Fascist.

Then he looked at his paper. Only the first and the last

177

had any answers. 'Gavin Blair Summers' at the top. 'Anti-Fascist' at the bottom. Its nakedness was really too absurd. He would have to invent some answers for the others.

'Come along, Comrade.' The sharp woman was at his side. 'Can't you read? What military experience have you had?' She was so fierce, disdainful and uncompromising that he stammered, 'None, I haven't had any.'

'Well, why do you come here wasting our time? Are you a Member?'

'No. I'm not.'

'Not even the Labour Party?' she said, looking at his form.

By this time he was simply confused and ashamed, wishing he had never come. Harry seemed to have deserted him, and in the atmosphere of the crowded room where untidiness, dirt and bustle seemed to proclaim that it was the centre of a fight being waged against lack of money, stupidity and time, he saw himself as useless, a waster. The overworked woman's irritation he took as purely personal contempt. The only thing he wanted was to escape.

Another worker who had collected the rest of the forms was reading his blank paper over his shoulder.

'Well, I don't see it's the least use *your* coming back tomorrow. You can if you like. But I can tell you it won't be any good. You can't *do* anything,' the woman concluded.

'Perhaps he can drive,' the other one suggested more kindly.

'Yes, I can drive,' Gavin said, pathetically eager, 'and I can type,' as if this might be an exculpation for his other huge sins of omission.

'Ever drive a lorry?' the woman said, half turning as she was going away. 'And can you *mend* one? We don't
178

want people unless they're really some use. Still, I'll put it in.' She added the last qualification as if it were a mitigation which she didn't really think would alter the sentence.

Gavin was only anxious to get outside. Harry and his friend Bill, and the others had handed in their forms, had received their appointments for tomorrow. They were talking excitedly about the future. They barely noticed Gavin.

'We'll show the . . . bastards where they get off, eh Harry?' Bill was saying. 'This is going to be a hell of a show. Christ Almighty, us four again. The bloody . . . will run like . . .! We'll show 'em.'

'Let's have a drink and celebrate,' Harry suggested, and turning to Gavin, 'Coming, Gavin?'

'No, I'm not.'

'Oh, come on and have a drink. There's plenty of time.'

'No, I don't think I will.'

'All right, see you here tomorrow?'

'No, I don't think I'm coming.'

'For God's sake, why not?'

They turned and walked a little distance from the others who were laughing and talking on the pavement. Gavin dramatised his self-pity.

'They don't want me and I suppose they're quite right. I'm no bloody good to them. I've got nothing to offer. I can't do anything. What good would I be? Didn't you see? . . . No, you were too busy. I couldn't fill in the form. There wasn't anything for me to say.'

Harry was rather contrite: 'It'll be all right, Gavin. That Comrade was just rushed, that's all. You come along tomorrow. They'll want you all right. Come on and have a drink.'

'No, I won't, Harry, you go on. See you in the morning.'

And filled with self-pity Gavin turned away and went off, feeling thoroughly excluded.

[The following was evidently my own recollection of their last days in England.]

Gavin wasn't, as he feared he might be, rejected. He was accepted, but told that with his lack of experience he would probably be kept at the base. There, his driving and his typing would come in useful. He felt it as a slur, but also hoped that Harry was right in saying that, once there, everything would be different. Harry, of course, had been accepted without reservations: his military background ensured that. It was after these two had joined that Pugh persuaded Harry to take him round and get him accepted, too. Harry needed little persuasion. Having taken the decision, he was in that euphoric state where the more the merrier seemed to him to be the right principle. They were doing the right, the only thing. They were the new heroes, and swaggered round in the intervening week left to them—or Pugh and Harry, anyhow, swaggered, with Gavin one cynical pace behind them.

In this mood they were impossible to reason with, and though Martin had not given up hope that he could win Harry round eventually, this proved illusory. Harry existed in a state of exultation miles above reason. Even Gavin was excited in a frightened sort of way, but anyhow for him there was the consolation that he was restored to Pugh's favours. And Pugh, who had sworn us all to silence until the actual departure, took the whole thing as a wonderful prank he was playing on Authority. 'It's better than last time,' he said to Gavin, displaying his indifference to which side he joined. 'Now there are three of us!'

They had one week's grace and they lived it up appropriately. I don't know what unpaid bills Pugh left behind at the Gargoyle. But Harry was the most extraordinary. It was as if he had a reversal to his Guards period, as if, in some way, he now regarded that as the 'real' part of his life, and all that had followed since, all his life with

180

Martin, had been a bad dream that he was delighted to have finished and done with. Now he was linking up again with the past, with the real life he ought never to have left. He saw a great deal of the ex-Guards pals he had met at the recruiting centre; and he seemed to coarsen visibly day by day.

Seeing him with these tough ex-soldiers, we could glimpse how he might have been before he met Martin. We remembered, of course, that capacity of his for taking on the colour of his environment; and with these Guards friends he was hearty, aggressive, coarse, damn-everybody, fuck-the-world, as if he had never been the essentially gentle, warm, cosy, intimate person we had come to know.

Martin despaired of him. He realised, too, that his disapproval of the whole venture was dampening what had become a riotous week of 'leave', to be spent in the traditional celebrations before death and danger closed in. He didn't mean to spoil their fun, but just couldn't help it, his long, sensitive face growing longer and more drawn as the week went by. He derived what comfort he could from the sight of this new-old Harry re-emerging.

'Perhaps, you see, he really is that kind of person at heart. Perhaps it is true that the life I led him into simply corrupted the one hard streak in him and made him soft all through. He is soft, and I had come to think wholly soft, incorrigibly lazy, self-indulgent and dependent. But perhaps there really is a toughness there that will face up to things and get him through, at least as long as these friends of his are around. I just hope there is, that's all. Because if there isn't, he's going to get the most awful shock when the reality hits him. And that's really the question, will he stand up to it? I would have said before, that he couldn't. Now I'm not so sure. Perhaps, some saving instinct has reasserted itself and knows what it is doing. Perhaps this will really be the saving of him.'

Gavin, on the other hand, found this new streak in Harry intolerable.

'He's really awful,' he told me, 'when he's out with those characters. He reverts to the primitive. Every other adjective is "fucking". He damns, with them, all intellectuals and queers. They are like some awful sub-parody of Kipling's *Soldiers Three*, drinking their way through a foreign port inhabited by natives—that is, civilians—whom they despise *en bloc*, and prophesying for themselves a world of fun and whoring which is how they view Spain through the mists of innumerable milds and bitters. Our old Harry has simply disappeared, merged into this conglomerate of tough and sweaty maleness. Fortunately Pugh finds them intolerable, too. So we have been thrown together again. My mother spends all her days in tears, a Niobe weeping only for herself. Martin? I can hardly see him. Refusing to accept the inevitable, he goes on and on and on, rehearsing the reasons why it's bound to end in disaster. He's probably quite right. But that's not what I want to hear at the moment. I wish the week was up.'

The week soon was up, anyhow, and our three shabby recruits set off. By arrangement, we none of us went to the station. These three were now anyhow wholly separated from us, the stay-at-homes, bound in their own fellowship of the future whatever it might turn out to be.

Author's Note

My special assignment had been to take the news round to Lady Nellie, and I wasn't looking forward to that. She was, not unnaturally, astonished at this turn in Pugh's political coat—for she still could hardly conceive of anyone not acting out of political conviction. But eventually, after a morning's argument, she came to see it, and after ringing her brother David and getting herself heartily abused, though it had really been in no sense her doing, she determined on a plan. She would go and put the case to the Communist Party themselves. After all, she had some pull there. And they must surely recognise the absurdity of the situation when it was only a month or so back that the boy had tried to join the Carlists? They were reasonable people— wasn't that the whole point of them? They would understand at once that this was a quite different case. They would get him sent back from Paris or straight from Spain. She would pay the expenses.

Nothing I said would deter her. She completely persuaded herself that reason was on her side, and that reason would prevail with the Communists above everyone. She persuaded me to accompany her after lunch to their headquarters in King Street. And I find in my files this record of our encounter:

We marched in, and Nellie promptly demanded to see Harry Pollitt and was scornfully asked who she thought she was.

'I'm Lady Nellie Griffiths, and you've been happy enough to use my name often enough. He'll know it if you don't.'

The formidable upper-class manner had some effect even here, and the complaining woman who had received us shuffled off inside. We were passed through two tough-minded subordinates and Nellie intimidated both of them. In this mood she was simply not to be stopped. 'If he won't come out to see me, I'll just sit here till he does. I thought we were supposed to be democratic. Is he too grand to see me?'

'Too busy,' they corrected her, and indeed she never got beyond his second-in-command, a large, tough, rangy man with a boxer's face who plainly despised her, and abruptly and rudely told her that Pollitt was off to a meeting, and he himself was leaving for Spain the next day. If what she had to say was important, he would listen, but for God's sake not to waste his time.

She explained about Pugh, and his attempt to join the Carlists, and his rebellion against his father.

The man listened impatiently to her somewhat muddled story and then wearily asked:

'Do you really think we can bother ourselves about individuals at this stage?'

This appalled her. She worried intensely about individuals, and she was to mull over this phrase for many months to come in a crisis of conscience.

184

'But Pugh is only a boy,' she cried. 'He isn't eighteen yet.'

'He can squeeze a trigger,' said the man dismissingly.

'And he isn't one of us at all . . .'

'Are you one of us, Lady Nellie . . . really one of us . . . if you can come here at this juncture trying to weaken our forces?'

'But he'll be no good to you. He's just an anarchist. I told you, he tried to join the Carlists.' Lady Nellie was getting hysterical and muddled.

The man smiled ironically: 'The harsh realities may bring about a conversion. Who knows?'

Nellie was driven back to threats.

'If this story of your taking a boy—and this boy especially, son of a Minister—gets into the papers, how would we like that?'

The man gave his iron smile again: 'Presumably we don't intend betraying the Party by giving it to the papers, do we?'

'No—but his father might—or anyone.'

'Let them. We shall deny it, if it suits us, and call it Fascist propaganda.'

'But you know it's true!'

'The truth is there to be used, Lady Nellie. We might, on the other hand, turn it to our advantage. Now I must go. I am very busy.'

'So you'll let this silly boy be killed?'

'Now, look here, Lady Nellie,' the man said sternly, 'hundreds of thousand of silly boys are being killed on either side at this very moment. This is war, not family games. You bourgeois all think you can make the rules to suit yourselves. You're all romantics. That boy has volunteered. That boy has been accepted. That boy will take his chance like everyone else. It doesn't matter to us that his father's an Earl and a Junior Minister—except in so far as we can use that to help the cause. We are all of us valuable only in so far as we are useful. You, too, Lady Nelli Now will you excuse me?'

There was plainly nothing more to be done and we filed disconsolately out, and made our way protesting to Martin's. We found him in not much of a mood for offering sympathy. He was too preoccupied with his own worry about Harry. Indeed their conversation resembled a duet in which each were playing not quite the same but similar tunes, but in quite different and dissimilar keys.

'You see, if only I hadn't ever taken Harry on he never would have been interested in Spain one way or the other. I can't deny my responsibility.'

'But what does one care about,' wailed Nellie, 'if one doesn't care about individuals? What's it all about, if not to see that individuals have a better chance of a better life?'

'Yet I'm certain, too,' Martin went on with his own line of thinking,' that I brought out something really valuable in Harry. I'm sure that my Harry—our Harry—was a better person than the Harry those yobs know. Surely it must be, isn't it?'

'But he's only a boy!' Lady Nellie had reverted to Pugh. 'At seventeen one's capable of any silliness. Surely we ought to have some responsibility for children?'

'What I do realise,' Martin said, 'is that Harry isn't just one person—almost isn't a person at all. One sees that now. He is just what his surroundings make him. If everyone is brave, he'll be brave; but if anyone panics, he'll panic. He isn't fit for it, you know, he really isn't.'

And so they went on talking at cross purposes, then and for many days afterwards.

SPANISH FILE IV

LETTERS FROM THE FRONT

From Gavin

Here we are in Albacete after a nightmare journey. I, anyhow, thought it was a nightmare, though Harry and his gang seemed to have enjoyed it in a drunken sort of way. But we were the oddest collection you ever saw. There were about a dozen of us from London. The others were mostly the sort of dedicated young men from the lesser suburbs that you meet at demos and Cell meetings, frightfully disapproving of Harry and his gang, but themselves a little scared, I guess, below the dedication. At Paris we picked up a mixed international lot, French, Germans, Hungarians, all sorts, and they were much better, taking everything much more in their stride, and singing endless songs to a mouth-organ. But it was awfully tiring on those hard wooden benches all the way through France, and we got hungry and thirsty and irritable.

Albacete is a dull, flat, monochrome country town in a huge, dry, dusty plain. And offers little in the way of distraction, which is going to try the Guardsmen high. Harry and the gang are as insupportable as ever, Harry as bad as any of them—worse in some ways. At every wayside station they jumped out and pursued any girl in sight with wolf-whistles and obscenities, and assured each other that all the French girls wanted nothing else but *that*. I cringed in shame for my countrymen, and so did Pugh. Why is every Englishman, loose abroad, so absolutely odious? And they haven't at all got the knack of being friendly with the other nationalities. They patronise them as if Bill and Harry and their friends thought themselves infinitely superior. Horrid! And to think the Comrades are always extolling the virtues of the working classes! Nothing but boorish pigs, really. Here at Albacete they are on the rampage, looking for women and finding none, and so furious with everyone.

We're just sorting ourselves and kitting ourselves out in an odd-job lot of uniforms. Hours and hours of standing about in queues, and some very officious officer 'Comrades' who look right bastards to me, ordering us officiously about. Not much equality and democratic discipline in our army, I guess.

'Shades of the prison house.' I feel that old school feeling coming on. It's very like being back there and no way out. We shall see.

Love,
Gavin.

From Harry to Martin

Well, we've made a good start. The journey was great fun. The boys were in fine form and kept our spirits up all the way (except for Gavin, who seemed to be rather down in the mouth). At Paris a whole contingent of International Comrades joined us, and we sang our way all the length of France. Do you remember those songs, rather nostalgic but still somehow hopeful, that they used to sing in Vienna? There were lots of those; and everyone was sharing out salami and bread and beer, and we really all felt *one*.

By the time we got to Albacete we really were a single body. That's the difference, you see, Martin, about this war. We weren't just a lot of conscripts going where we were told to go. Being volunteers makes all the difference. We were all united with the same purpose. It's a lovely feeling. And we must cling on to it.

I think where Gavin feels rather out of it is that he's too individualistic. He doesn't seem to have this same lovely feeling we all have of being a Unity. It's the bourgeois upbringing, I suppose, because Pugh is really rather the same. I'm working-class like the others; and it all comes back to me, my childhood, I mean, how my father and all the other miners felt bound together by being the same. They may have been oppressed, but it was the great compensation, this feeling of togetherness. It's tremendously strong here. And makes everything seem all right.

I used to wonder whether the Comrades didn't put too much emphasis on being working-class. After all, all of you seemed to live much better lives than we did. But I see now that they were right. It's your lives that are the illusion, and the real thing, the thing that matters, is the working-class unity. It makes me very proud to be one of them. And as we're all here of our own free will to get this thing finished, that makes a tremendous difference, too. Of course we grumble and complain and get browned off, like everyone else. So much army routine is time-wasting, isn't it? Or seems so. But it has to be done, hasn't it? And because we are what we are, we can put up with it much better.

You see it isn't really like being in the army like the Guards was. It's more being a kind of fellowship. We don't do all the unpleasant things that have to be done just because we're barked at. We know they have to be done and we know why, and so we're ready enough to do them, however boring they are, kit parades and all that preliminary organising.

I'm not sure, though, that all the Comrade officers at this base really remember it. Some of them seem too ready to forget what we are—volunteers. Well, it's our business to remind them, isn't it? This is a real democratic army and that's something quite different, isn't it?

Let me hear from you,

Harry.

From Gavin

Back at school, back at school, back at dreary old bloody old school! That's what we used to chant on the first day of term, and the chant is singing in my head. I'm in the office, terribly inefficient it is, too. I type out 'requisitions' for equipment which never comes and letters to the Comrades at home full of revolutionary phrases and black lies about how high morale is (which it isn't).

But it's very slack really. There isn't enough to do and I'm working hard on getting myself transferred to something more active. So is Pugh. He's with me in the office, but as he can't type, he does nothing except occasionally drive someone somewhere, which he likes. But he's very discontented. They've found out who he is, and mean not to let him get into any danger. The very serious Scotch second-in-command gave me a long paternal talk about him, how he was very young and my responsibility. Why *mine*, for God's sake? Anyhow, I've no control over him whatsoever.

I was supposed to explain to him that it was his comradely duty to put up with not being sent into the line. You can imagine how much feeling of 'comradely duty' one can inspire in Pugh!

There's a lot of talk of 'Comrades' and 'comradely' here, but the reality is the duty, not the 'comradely'. The 'Comrade' officers and the 'Comrade' commissars are all like the worst kind of schoolmasters—the ones who put you on your honour not to do this or that. They don't talk about honour; they talk about 'comradely duty'—or 'socialist discipline', which means doing what you don't want to because you ought to. It's not going down too well with Harry's lot.

Discipline, in fact, is the great problem. They hold meetings to discuss it and the Scotch second-in-command preaches sermons to them; and is amazed that they don't respond. Harry is getting awkward, too. You know his wonderful theories about democratic discipline? Well, that seems to be all in the past; they have 'socialist' discipline now which doesn't seem to me to differ much from the naval discipline my father preaches. Harry, always one for an argument, stands up and spouts for the old democratic kind and won't be taught the new.

I happen to know they are building a prison at the moment. That'll teach socialist discipline all right.

For the evenings there are two cafés; both equally depressing. In one the French play dominoes; in the other the Germans play chess. Harry's lot can't find any girls. But they have found Pugh.

Love,
Gavin.

From Harry to Martin

We are in a rather difficult stage here now, partly because there isn't really enough to do and nothing to do it with. We have an odd-job lot of uniforms, but no arms, and it's hard to get toughs like us to take arms drill seriously with broomsticks. Besides, we know all that. It's the real practice with rifles we need, and there aren't any.

All the equipment there was has gone up to the front lines, where the Brigades who came out before us have taken over a sector of the line. Here, at the base, they are very proud of that, and we hear that they are doing very well. All I can say is that that first lot must have been better trained than we're being.

What really worries me here, Martin, is the attitude of the Comrade officers and commissars. They seem entirely to have forgotten all the principles that are supposed to work in a democratic army. They've coined this new phrase 'socialist discipline', which just means what the Guards meant, by another name. Some of us are trying to re-educate them back into remembering what democratic discipline means, but it's uphill work. They always think they know best.

I wonder if you can't do anything your end to get some proper Comrade sent out here. It's very urgent. I mean a Comrade who knows what this is all about and how it should be done. These Comrade officers are putting every-one's back up because they're acting just like old army people. Someone ought to be sent out to see what's going on. Otherwise there's going to be trouble, I can tell you.

Can't Pollitt be persuaded to come? I think you should tell him, I really do, how bad morale is getting. He'd see at once that you can't treat Comrades the way you do men in the Guards. It just won't work. We've held several meetings to discuss it. But unfortunately we aren't quite unanimous. The Germans are the trouble. I sometimes think all Germans are crypto-Fascists. They positively like being ordered about. And there are a great many of them.

What are we to do, Martin? Things are pretty bad. We've decided we won't obey silly orders we don't agree with and see what happens. But Gavin, down at base, tells me they've turning one building into a military prison. Does that sound like 'socialist' discipline to you?

You see we're quite ready to co-operate by obeying when the orders are sensible. You've got to have some sort of discipline. We quite see that. But when orders are just silly, surely the whole point of a democratic army is that you can say, why? But they won't hear of it!

Take this question of the broomsticks. What's the good of me, Bill and Bert and the others spending *whole mornings* and *whole afternoons* learning elementary arms drill with broomsticks when we've been through the Guards? Surely we could be doing something more useful? But they won't listen. They say we can set the example. But you can see it's silly. You can't do it with broomsticks, anyhow, and the intructors don't know anything. I should have thought Bert would be the person to teach. But instead of drawing on our experience—all the various experiences of the various Comrades—and letting us teach each other, they've gone right back to authoritarianism, and all doing the same thing at once.

They gave us a great lecture on how the Anarchists, who do have a democratic army, had let the Republic down with their lack of discipline in the line: and how it was up to us to show the natives what socialist discipline could do. But I'm with the Anarchists every time. What's the point of being here, if we're just to be ordinary cannon-fodder like any other army? Do write to me, Martin, and do try and get someone *with real authority* sent out to report on the situation. Otherwise I don't know what may happen.

As ever,
Harry.

Our trouble is that us who think like this are badly out-numbered, and they can always turn to the others—Germans and so on—and say, Look at them! They're mucking in, why can't you? But it's the principle of the thing, isn't it? You do see that?

G   193

Oh, it's so dreary here. You can't imagine. There's simply nothing to do. I don't mind doing nothing all day in the office: we can gossip and drink a foul sort of coffee and pretend to be busy. But the evenings are hell. I wish I could get drunk as most others do. But I've never been able to, and anyhow the supplies are running out. You can imagine the row that's causing with Bert and them. There are just these two cafés, and some very thin wine, and some very weak beer, sometimes. And the same old people. We shan't get leave for ages, they say, and they also say that the cafés may be 'out of bounds' four days a week. I wonder who 'they' are. 'They' are always saying this or that. They say the war's going very badly; but the war hardly affects us. We don't seem to be in a war. We're more like in some concentration camp that one's read about in Germany, and the 'Comrades' don't seem all that different from the SS.

Harry is having a very severe and very, very boring *crise de conscience*. It goes on day after day. He simply can't understand why he can't do as he likes, and is convinced if he were running the camp everything would be quite different. I dare say it would, but I doubt myself if it would be better, except, of course, that it simply couldn't be worse.

The real trouble is, I think, that we're kind of 2nd class Brigaders. The first-class ones are the ones who came out at the beginning and are now up there at the Front. We are constantly having our noses rubbed in their virtues, how splendid and disciplined they were compared to us; and their doings and sayings are for ever being rammed down our throats. But that—and they—was before the days of organisation. Everything was improvised, and in a spirit of wild optimism. Our second wave has come in at a time when things aren't going so well, and also when the best officers and NCO's have already gone up into the line. We're left with the officious second best who are conscious of their second bestness and try to make up for it with officiousness.

Gavin.

From Harry

A disgusting thing happened last week. I was given two days in the cells. Yes, they've got their cells now just like any capitalist army. Wooden bench. Bucket in corner. Foul smell all day. Only one meal—beans in water.

It happened like this. We were on parade at six in the morning as usual, and as usual we did some futile marching up and down for an hour and a half with our silly broomsticks. At breakfast there wasn't enough coffee, and it was cold and we were fed up. The night before we'd had this meeting, and we'd decided that if the training didn't get better, we'd make a stand. There's a German Comrade, Hans, whose very good at fieldcraft, and Bert knows a good deal about machine-gun siting. Why couldn't we split into two, and half of us learn from each? But the trouble is that Bainter—our Comrade under-officer—doesn't know about either, and thinks it would be bad for discipline if he isn't the one in charge. So at the after breakfast parade, as per arrangement, I took a step forward and said, 'Comrade Bainter, I've a suggestion to make.'

'I don't want your suggestions, Comrade,' he said. 'Get back into your ranks.'

I stood my ground and went on. 'This is supposed to be a democratic army, Comrade. Oughtn't you to listen to my suggestions?'

'This is a socialist army, Comrade,' he said, 'and socialist

195

discipline demands that you obey orders. Get back into your ranks.'

'Crap on your socialist army,' suddenly Bert says, taking a pace forwards. 'Do we want to be trained or don't we?' There were a lot of murmurs from the rest. Bainter was as red as a beetroot with fury but managed to control himself. 'I'll give you both one more chance. Get back into your ranks.'

But we stood our ground, and he had to go and bring out Seton, the Scotch second-in-command. He gave us the usual lecture on socialist discipline and then put Bert and me under arrest. Another lecture about how we weren't in an Anarchist militia, but in a proper socialist army, and orders had to be obeyed first and discussed afterwards. And we each had two days cells.

I'm fed up. We aren't being trained and we're being treated like thugs, not like reasonable men. If we are ever sent into the line, I wouldn't like to be Bainter with Bert gunning for him.

Can't anything be done for us? I feel we're rotting out here. Rotting and forgotten. Does anyone at home remember us? Parcels would be a help. Chocolate, things like that. The food is terrible and getting worse. *There are rumours today of our being sent forward.* But what use should we be? We're an ill-trained, ill-disciplined, rebellious rabble.

DO SOMETHING.

Harry.

Later

We've been let down again by the others. When Bert and I came out of our cells, we called a meeting to discuss the situation, and would you believe it, we were voted down. I can't make it out. The others must know how bad our training has been, though perhaps not having been in the

Guards, like us, they don't fully appreciate it. But we know, and we know how hopeless we would be if we were sent into the line like this. But they wouldn't listen, and there's a lot of talk now of our being sent forward some time very soon. Of course, being voted down, we couldn't do anything. That is democracy, isn't it? But we're going to keep on, just the same, trying to win votes for our way. Because, of course, we're right even if the others don't know it. They'll find out all right when they get there—and then it'll be too late.

From Gavin

It's all started. A week ago the others suddenly moved off. We didn't know where, but we could guess why and, sure enough, last night some of the wounded came back. They'd been given rifles of sorts and pushed into the line to plug a gap, and told they must hold on to it for a bit until reserves came up, when they'd be pulled out and trained properly. But they're still there. Two of Bert's friends were killed. Harry was among those who came back. He wasn't actually wounded. But he's in a pretty bad way. They call it 'battle fatigue'. Better tell Martin.

Later

Crisis! Saw Harry in hospital. He's in a bit of a jam. It seems he just came down with the wounded without orders, complaining of 'terrible pains in the stomach'. He said it had been an absolute shambles. We clashed with the Moors on the hill, and lost hundreds of men. Two of Bert's pals were shot at his side. When the clash was over, the wounded were left lying out in the middle and they could hear them groaning and crying out for help all night.

Harry was absolutely shaken to the core and couldn't stand it. Great fuss at the office about him and several others, how they are to be treated, etc. Various views from 'Shoot them', to 'Pretend it didn't happen'. But at the moment everyone's too busy worrying over the military disaster, which is about what it's been. Luckily a reserve battalion of Germans—the best fighters of all—was standing by and they were put in behind ours to take over from us.

Of course, the fact is that this running of things by the Communist Party is a silly way of doing it. Ours just don't know enough to do it properly. And they know it really. That's why they may not take too grave a view of Harry. They know they're guilty men too.

Harry's quite cracked up, tell Martin. I'll get this to you as soon as I can.

Pugh and I are quite determined to get away from this place where we're just kept hanging about doing nothing useful. We want to get somewhere where they're less incompetent than they are here—my God, they're incompetent. We have a plan that should get us into the war. By the time you get this we probably won't be here.

Gavin.

From Harry to Martin

I'm in a real jam now, Martin, I really am. Gavin is going to get this letter out to you. I've had it, and I'm not going back into the line whatever they do. I won't. They can do what they like. I'm ill. I really am. I couldn't do any more.

It happened ten days ago. We were suddenly paraded and told we were going up the line at once. We collected our gear and set off, on foot of course, with a few lorries for our heavy stuff. We marched about fifteen miles that day and we hadn't done any real route marching so everyone's feet were in ribbons. There were no proper arrangements for food, but we were fairly cheerful, thinking we were going to do something at last. We slept out at a farm and some of us got into the barns and it wasn't too bad. But there was this feeling of nothing being properly organised.

The next morning we hung about for two or three hours after reveille and at last a string of lorries came and took us up to the rear lines. This was on the lower slopes of the hill, and when we got out there were these bullets making a little 'phit' as they went over, and we were all ducking. But they told us these were just the spent ones and didn't matter. You didn't hear the one that got you.

We were in reserve there for two or three days. That's when we got our rifles, but we didn't have any chance of practising with them. You could see the front lines at the top of the hill. The men in fox-holes and slit trenches, and we did get on to making some of those. Then one evening the alarm came: firing had broken out everywhere. Wounded came streaming back and we were led up the hill. And over the top there were the enemy, dreadfully close. Moors! And the clatter of machine guns and the hell of a racket from grenades. We hadn't any; just these old rifles and an incompetent officer.

That first wave of the attack had been halted and we were waiting for another. It came just before nightfall. Wave after wave of these Moors coming at us, and we firing these old rifles which didn't seem to stop anything. We didn't stay long up there. Any of us. We were half way down that hill in no time. An officer rushed up and ordered us back, waving his pistol. But what could we do? We were back in the reserve lines again. It was a real panic.

Luckily someone else halted the Moors or they didn't

dare come on alone through that gap. The firing died down and we were rounded up again for the night. And all night between us and them the wounded were crying out 'Comrades! Help, Comrades!' in every language and we were warned not to do anything—because if the Moors do get you you've had it. Firing went on all night, and these cries, until Bill and Sam said they were going to do something and they began crawling forward out of the slit trench and were both shot instantly. They can see in the dark, those Moors. We got them back in, and Sam was dead, right between the eyes. Bill seemed less bad: but he was in pain all night.

At first light, I and another Comrade got him down to the reserve, and below that there were some ambulances. We went right down to the road and put him in, and there were a lot of others, too. And I just couldn't go back. I just couldn't. I had this awful pain in my guts. And so I just stayed in the ambulance and we were driven back here.

I don't know what happens to me now. Just have to see. But I'm not going back. Not up there again, whatever they do.

There's something else rather serious. Gavin and Pugh have decided to take off. They won't say where. But they're going. By the time you get this, they'll be gone, and God knows what will happen to them either, cos things are getting tough round here tonight. Everyone's in a panic. Everyone's blaming everyone else and they're talking of shooting all deserters.

But they really are going. Better tell Nellie and see if she can do something—or God knows what will happen to them. God knows what'll happen to me!

Harry.

PART FIVE

Rescue Work

Author's Note

The arrival of these last letters caused a flurry of activity. Both Martin and Lady Nellie had already been invited to go to Spain to do propaganda work, and both had been contemplating it. Now they each decided to set things moving and get out there as quickly as possible. Martin, with typical clear-sightedness, had one primary aim—to get to Albacete as quickly as he could, and try to sort out Harry's mess.

Nellie was less single-minded. She naturally didn't feel over Pugh the same guilt or even responsibility that Martin felt over Harry. But she had hopes she might be able to do something—she didn't quite know what. And over Spain itself she retained her romanticism. Pugh apart, she wanted to see it, to be there at the living centre of the most vivid historical moment of our times. She even believed that once there she might find herself some niche where she could be useful.

For her, helping—or trying to help—Pugh was only an incidental, while for Martin the rescue of Harry was a primary objective. He didn't mean to waste more time than he had to on broadcasting or reporting. That could come afterwards if he succeeded in his first aim.

Nellie, being a Party member, was the first to go, and she went on a rising tide of high excitement, an excitement which only grew as the kind of expectations she had of the atmosphere there were confirmed in everything she saw and experienced:

FROM NELLIE'S DIARY

Arrived at Barcelona after a thrilling journey. Must get it all down so that I'll know what to say when I broadcast tomorrow. It all started the moment we crossed the frontier. There you enter a quite new world. All across the channel and down through France is our well-known weary world of today, the people grim, silent, dull, unmoved. And then the moment you cross the frontier at Port Bou, you're in this totally different ebullient world, the world of tomorrow. Life bursting out on every side, a marvellous exuberance and *élan*, as if the top had been blown off the pan and the boiling water was bubbling over. It's intoxicating. By the end of a day I was drunk with it.

At first, few signs of the war. Anarchist guards at the frontier in their Anarchist uniforms—blue denim overalls, belts, revolvers and the forage caps set at an angle on their heads. They were very strict about papers, and two volunteers were sent back, though they wept and pleaded to come in. They have to be careful about spies. My papers were passed at once with fat and friendly grins, and I was sent to the bureau on the station presided over by the local Railwaymen's Syndicate. Everything run by the Trade Unions—or Syndicates as the Anarchists call them. They looked at my papers and then gave me a free pass to Barcelona. I thought it was a ticket and bourgeois-conditioned, tried to pay. They were really shocked! Things aren't run like that. The railways are there for those who have business to use them. And if you have business, you travel free! Real Socialism at last.

A few rather un-military-looking soldiers about, and some in bandages to remind us of the realities. Everywhere

204

these lovely posters we've seen some examples of in England. But lots more. Beautiful, simple, stark. And all those confusing initials on them. FAI, CNT, UGT, POUM, PSU, all standing for the different parties of the Popular Front.

The train didn't start for ages. I was one of the first in, but the carriage—one of those long open carriages with wooden benches—slowly filled up to overflowing. Soon packed with a whole variety of people. Volunteers—one French who had been home on leave and put me in the picture—returning militia-men, and peasants. And we rumbled slowly off.

The peasants predominated with their tightly filled string bags and heavy parcels, getting in and out at every station—and we stopped, it seemed, almost as much as we went. At every little wayside halt. The peasants looked suspicious to me at first and didn't join in all the laughter and chatter that was generated by the Anarchists and militia-men.

Those last were wonderful. No one could be more gay and kindly than they were, helping the old peasant women in and out at each stop, scrupulously respecting anyone's right to a seat if they'd left it unguarded for a moment, insisting on sharing out any standing that had to be done; and even deciding that any foreigners must have seats even if this meant their standing all the way. Then they passed round their wine-skins and bread and sausage, and were positively insulted if you refused to take your share. And all the time laughing and singing, cracking jokes, shouting to each other like the happiest of happy children.

They jumped down at every station, they waved and shouted to the girls. They came back carrying more sausages, more wine, coffee, cognac, cigarettes which they shared all round. I tried to get out and contribute some, but they wouldn't let me. 'Ladies don't buy, ladies take.' Oh, it was exhilarating! They picked the wayside flowers, forget-me-nots, primroses, violets and decorated my hair and everybody else's. They shouted to each other, pointing out the beauty of the blossom. They were overwhelming in their generosity and high spirits.

Talking to my Frenchman I wondered why the peasants joined in so little, and he said, had I noticed their age? Their sons and the younger men were all at the war and these were the elder people and there was the clean-cut line, he said, between the generations. The elder peasants viewed the whole spectacle of the war with suspicion. They'd seen it happen before, only to be crushed in the end—which this certainly won't be. It couldn't be. When you see this excited quality of sheer living, you know they couldn't lose, couldn't ever go back to the old ways.

But the old peasants viewed it like spectators watching a show which they enjoyed but weren't taking part in. Even when they did join in the jokes and the singing and the ragging, they were somehow aloof. Like grown-ups called in to play with the children, they tried to come down to the child level, but never succeeded in throwing themselves into it, because they can't believe it will last. They aren't disapproving or hostile, as the older generation is when the young are enjoying themselves. They're just half-hearted, as if they knew from experience that the game will come to an end and—like many children's games—end in tears.

That was the Frenchman's explanation, and I think it rather good. With the younger men, it isn't a game at all. It's a deadly serious business, but conducted with panache. Panache is what these Anarchists marvellously have. They were laughing, but not playing. They feel their destiny is in their own hands and failure to grasp it means almost certain death, actual or spiritual. Between the laughing and the singing they make this quite clear. They've turned their

206

world upside down—they're no longer sat upon by the bosses, the priests and the landlords. They're on top now, controlling their own lives, and responsible for the future.

So they're living at their very best as human beings—and what a wonderful best it is. They've got their quite brand-new set of values, generosity, comradeship, the cause. The old values, work-for-money, insecurity for lack of money, have dropped away. There's just themselves with their natural national gift for living, for immediately enjoying the fact of being alive and in control.

Barcelona province is the stronghold of the Anarchists, of course, and this ebullience, my Frenchman says, is a special Anarchist thing. And he says that they are too spiritual, really. The importance of *materiel*, of money, arms, munitions, supplies, gets rather left out in this feeling of pure freedom. They haven't fully got down to the problems of organisation while they're still enjoying the intoxication of having delivered themselves from the old cramping moulds in which they were strait-jacketed.

Perhaps that's true. I don't know. What I do know is that never in my wildest dreams have I imagined that life could be as perfect as this glimpse of freedom on that train. It was so spontaneous, so all-pervasive, so natural and with a gaiety beyond description. Life fairly flowed; no, it crackled, like electricity in the hair—crisp, clean, fresh.

And when at last we got to Barcelona, there was the same feeling there. The whole town had been taken over by the same spirit of absolute freedom—freedom pure and unalloyed. The crowds walking up and down the broad pavements are alight with it—the girls all with beautifully dressed hair, the men and boys each with a revolver on his hip, dressed mostly in short leather jerkins. No hats for the women and leather jerkins for the men seems the correct revolutionary dress. There are no rich sections and no poor sections, rich cafés and poor cafés. The town's all one, taken over entire by the proletariat.

Instead of vulgar advertisements, these wonderful posters everywhere. All the smart hotels have been taken over by the different political parties. Trams clang up and down the streets with people clinging on like bees, and no inspectors to turn them off or conductors to shout 'No more! Full up!' In the cafés the waiters disdain to take tips. Loudspeakers high up in the square dispense martial music or news. Everywhere this gaiety of laughing, this electrical excitement.

While I was sitting in a café, a band came down the street playing the Internationale, and it didn't sound priggish and forced as it does in England. There were thirty or forty recruits marching behind and the crowds swarmed across and cheered them with the clenched fist salute, and the last two of the recruits, mere boys, left the ranks and, coming together as for a dance, waltzed down the street.

This is everything we've all worked for, everything we've dreamed about in our Cell meetings and our Demos— so drab and dull as they were. But they've flowered here and blossomed into a perfect world.

Later

Oh dear, I've done such an absurd thing. There's only one big hotel left open, the Ritz, and I wasn't going there! So I chose a bright little one in a side street. It seemed specially gay with lots of young couples going in and out. I thought it would suit me exactly! And it turned out, of course, to be a *maison de passe*! But it was quite all right. Clean and comfortable, and I was too tired to be kept awake by the comings and goings. Anyhow it suits me well, I say.

But my new English guide, Reg Arnold, is very dis-approving. He's altogether a rather disapproving young man. He was waiting for me at the Bureau for Foreigners
208

where I had to report. They were expecting me, and have laid on tours of hospitals and schools and rehabilitation centres which they're very proud of. Reg Arnold was studying in Barcelona when the uprising started and stayed on to give what help he could. He works partly at the Radio Station, partly as a guide for important foreigners.

There's a small group of four or five young English people who do this, and they took me out to coffee and then to lunch at the Communist Party Restaurant. Each Party and Trade Union has these communal restaurants where you get a good simple meal in exchange for a ration ticket. No money passes.

It felt very strange and exciting to be in an openly respected Communist Party headquarters. The restaurant is in the basement and seemed very well run—huge, too. The young English rather sniffy—they're altogether rather sniffy—when I described my journey. Of course, they're used to it all, and it no longer strikes them the same way. But I admire the way they live, between a small unheated *pensione* and the hotel which has been turned into the Radio Centre. They have a tiny salary each and have to go without coffee and go short on cigarettes if they want to go to the cinema. They're very dedicated.

In the evening I made my broadcast to the outside world and tried to convey what I had felt in the train. Afterwards Reg Arnold disapproved. He said I ought to have talked about the orphan school they had taken me to in the afternoon. I said I would when I had seen more.

But then he gave me what he called a severe warning. He said I was very unwise to praise the Anarchists at the moment. I told him it wasn't the Anarchists I was praising as such—just the spirit of the whole place.

'It amounts to the same thing,' he said very solemnly. 'Don't you realise that the Anarchists are really Social Fascists? We'—and by we he meant the Communists, for

209

the little English group are all Communists—'We are having great difficulties with them. And if you go praising them like that, you'll find yourself very unpopular, very unpopular indeed.'

So we had rather a set-to. Because nothing could have been more wonderful than those Anarchists on that train, and isn't there supposed to be a Popular Front of all the parties? Then he proceeded to explain that, though there was a Popular Front, what was important was that the best party ran it, and that was the Communists. I couldn't argue, not knowing anything about it. But it's rather taken the edge off things for me. Being in the hands of Communists I'm only shown Communist schools and so on, and when I asked to see the others, there was this shocked disapproval. And they spend all their time running down all the other Parties, and read you extracts from their newspapers, doing the same. They might almost be at war with the others, and the Anarchists especially. I don't understand it. Out on the streets there is this ecstatic feeling of the town being one great revolutionary experiment. Yet this little group spend all their time and energy disparaging it. I can't help thinking of Elvira and those Austrian Socialists and how they had come to mistrust the Communists. Now I begin to see why.

I've done three days looking at hospitals, etc., and two broadcasts. Martin arrives tomorrow, so everyone says. I look forward to seeing him.

FROM MARTIN'S DIARY

Arrived in Barcelona after an exhausting but exhilarating trip, exhilarating, that is, after we had passed the frontier. Marvellous spirit in the slow train coming along from Port

Bou. Revolution with the lid off, and spirits bubbling over. Met by a pursy-mouthed little group of English Commies, very puritan and very English, who had elaborate plans for me. But I mean simply to go to Albacete as soon as I can. I shall have to stay one day and do one broadcast first, I suppose. Realised from this pursy-mouthed little English group how tough it's going to be in Albacete.

Met Nellie in the evening who was bursting with a mixture of romanticism and disillusion. Romantic about the revolution, but disillusioned with this English group who have been looking after her and pumping her with anti-Anarchist propaganda. I can see she is going to get into great difficulties here. Romantics like her expect everyone on our side to be angelic. Can't get it into her head that being right doesn't make people any nicer—or being wrong any nastier. I know this kind of sour English Communist all too well and I expect they have their Spanish counterparts, too.

Still, I see what Nellie means. The contrast between their narrowness and the wonderful expansiveness you see in the streets is depressing. One can only hope they remain the small minority they are at present. Or are they? I had lunch with a Socialist Minister, and though he was very guarded I rather gathered that the CP is becoming something of a real menace—owing to the Russian support of them, of course, the *quid pro quo* that they exact for their not very plentiful supply of arms. I guess one had better keep as much out of internal politics as one can, if one doesn't want to be disillusioned. Equally, I don't think the war is going anything like as well as we thought in England. That's only a snap judgement. But I sense it. I stupidly said something of the kind to Nellie. She simply wouldn't, or couldn't, take it. But I think she'll have to get used to the fact.

I've put over a lot of stuff about wanting to have my first

contact with the English Brigade, so they're sending me
to Albacete tomorrow, and praising me for my patriotism!
I rather wish Nellie weren't coming, but she insists, and I
suppose she really does want to know about Pugh. But
she'll be no help.

Later

Yesterday, on the way to Albacete, they arranged our visit
to the front. A harrowing experience. And it wasn't just
funk, plain unvarnished funk, that made it harrowing. But
to be honest I must record that too. We drove out to the
base at the bottom of the famous hill that Harry described
in his letter and, as you climb up into the reserve trenches,
already the spent bullets are flicking past one, making one
duck humiliatingly at every other step. I didn't find it hard
to imagine the horror and confusion Harry described when
the enemy broke through. What I can't possibly imagine,
what is totally unimaginable for me, is to be stuck there,
bound as these men are to living in this danger day after
day, night after night. I quite simply couldn't do it. I
always knew this from the first, and refused to be trapped
into it back in England. But it shakes one all the same, to
come up against it so nakedly and so positively.

Just for this reason visiting it like this, a tourist, a sightseer, with the tourist's freedom to take the next car away
from it, is a kind of impertinence I was horribly conscious
of. What redeemed that was the welcome we were given.
It was soon clear from their warmth and gratitude that
the men here wanted our visit, took it as a gesture of
remembrance coming from that other world of home. To
them we weren't sightseers but symbols which proved they
were not forgotten, a link with the world they longed to
get back to, but had momentarily renounced. Proud of
themselves and the fact of their being there, they wanted

that recorded, or even just witnessed: we were witnesses, not tourists.

Nellie was magnificent, I must say. It was an extra something for them to have a handsome woman up there on that bleak hill, and one who was all enthusiasm and excitement. She fairly responded to their warmth. She had to be shown everything and insisted we be taken up to the front line to have a pot shot at the enemy. It was all just like what one had seen in films out of the last war, the olive trees torn and shattered by bullet or shell, the corpses between the armies, the stray shots, the enemy somewhere over there crouched in similar positions. I recognised it as if I had always known it, and known I must keep out of it. Our guides were touchingly careful to make us keep our heads down, as if, because we were visitors, we were more important than the mere cannon-fodder who remained there day in and day out. We fired a few rounds from a machine-gun and I aimed to miss. Who was I to intrude on this private affair between the two armies who were both more like each other than I was to either?

While Nellie, back down in the reserve trenches, was taking messages to deliver home, I was asked, as I knew German, to go on and visit the Thaelmann battalion who were on the flank of the English, and I stayed to lunch with them. Here there was, I couldn't help noticing, a rather different sort of spirit among the Brigaders. The English seemed to be, more than anything, resigned, resigned to sticking it out, because there they were and there they had to stay, and they accepted their obligation with the kind of playing-down jokes which the English tend to use to cope with discomfort.

The Germans had a different spirit which derived from their different background. They weren't, in the same way as the English, free volunteers from a secure background of home. They were volunteers from the hounded life of refugees. Here on this hill they felt themselves to be more fully alive, more complete human beings, than ever they had been in the poverty of Paris or the uncertainties of Prague. Their lives as exiles, hunted, despised, pushed about, had flowered now into the far greater freedom of the front line. Instead of fighting their enemy with pamphlets and illegal presses and secret meetings, they were facing him openly on this hill with rifles, of a kind, in their hands. Even if the odds seemed against them, at least they were there standing up to them, and this gave them an aggressive spirit which showed itself in quite different sorts of jokes. Theirs were about the poorness of the weapons, the weakness of their support, the need for tanks and guns and air-cover. Instead of the patient English grumbles, there was an impatient edge on their interchanges, the impatience of men who wanted to get to grips with the enemy and smash them back.

I couldn't, of course, enter into this, me, English and a visitor, and with a very different problem and a less heroic one obsessing my thoughts. But knowing the Germans and knowing what these men would have suffered, I admired from an envious distance their extraordinary spirit. To be whole-hearted is a blessing and I suppose I am doomed never to know it.

FROM MARTIN'S DIARY

Albacete

At Albacete we found Harry still in the camp, but Gavin and Pugh had indeed taken off, and been posted as deserters. Seton, the Scottish Commissar, was the same man to whom Nellie had protested in London, but she got no more change out of him now. Nor did she seem disposed to fight much.

He told her curtly that only Pugh's extreme youth could possibly save him from being shot if and when he was caught, and it might not, at that. And she accepted this as if it were right. Later in the evening I argued with her about it.

After all, we knew that Pugh and Gavin had only gone off because they were being kept at base out of danger. Danger was what they both wanted and, as Gavin hinted, what they'd gone off to find. Anyhow it was an obviously silly way to treat them to keep them down here in an office —it was asking for trouble. And typical of the unimaginativeness of people like this Seton. The thing is we mustn't grant them anything, whatever we happen to think privately. We've got to fight them every inch of the way, right or wrong.

I happen to think Harry's behaviour intolerable. Not that after our visit to the front I don't sympathise with him wholeheartedly on one plane. That he couldn't stand it, I'm not at all surprised, but he might show some awareness of the spot he's put us in, and some slight remorse for having landed himself in this mess. But when I saw him this evening there wasn't a sign of it. On the contrary, he was in his most exasperating and argumentative mood. The 'Comrades' still couldn't decide what was to be done with him. I'll tackle them tomorrow. At the moment he's just helping around the camp while they make up their minds. We had an absurd sort of conversation, going something like this:

'You realise what a spot you've put us all in, I suppose.'

'I don't see why. I'm not doing anyone any harm. In so far as I'm doing some quite useful jobs around the place, I'm a help, aren't I?'

'You can't expect them to see it quite like that, though.'

'I don't see why not. We're a democratic party, aren't we? Then we ought to be allowed the freedom of our opinions. That's what I say.'

'But you committed yourself to coming out here to fight, and now you won't.'

'I'm allowed to change my mind, aren't I? If you suddenly decided to fight after all, they'd let you, wouldn't they? Why can't they let me decide to be a pacifist? I am one. That's what I am.'

'You realise in any other army you'd have been shot out of hand?'

'But I didn't join "any other army" and I wouldn't have done—just for that reason. When I joined this one I thought it would be run reasonably, and it isn't.'

'I think they're being pretty reasonable, considering.'

'They want to send me to a glasshouse. Is that being reasonable?'

'It's better than being shot!'

'You don't understand anything, Martin. How could you? You don't know what it's been like out here. It's easy for you coming in from the outside, and just able to drift off again when you've had enough! But I'm here, and if I didn't stick to my guns, I'd be dead on that hill now. Is that what you want?'

I thought his choice of metaphor unfortunate, but was there any use in continuing the argument at all? 'I think you ought to show some remorse for the situation you've put us all in—if not to them at least to me.'

'I don't see it. I think I'm being perfectly logical. If they don't see it, it's because they won't, isn't it?'

'And what am I supposed to think?'

'I expect you think I've let you down. You always have been on the look-out for that, haven't you, ever since we've been together? But I don't care what you think, I'm sticking to my guns.'

Later

Conference with Seton and another Comrade officer over

Harry. The most hopeful thing is that they don't really know what to do about him—and have hesitated rather too long. They keep repeating that on the night of the disaster the officer would have been perfectly justified in shooting some of them then and there. But, of course, he hadn't. The battalion, except for four or five who made off, reformed and went up the hill again. The four or five who went off were posted as deserters and doubtless would be shot. But Harry hadn't been one of them. He had gone up the hill again with the rest. Only the next morning he had come down with the wounded, claiming he was ill. Was that desertion? Did that deserve shooting? Probably not, for he was still there. He wasn't deserting. He was just refusing to go up into the line again. That was refusing to obey orders, they said (quite rightly), and you could be shot for that.

But the very fact that they were talking about it like this showed that they weren't in fact going to do it. It was too late. But they still wanted to do something as drastic as they dared.

I pressed the point that he might really be ill, he might have a stomach ulcer, for instance. But they replied that whether ill or not he still refused ever to take up a rifle again. What could they do with a Comrade who obstinately proclaimed his pacifism in the face of their arguments? There were penal establishments to which such people could be sent, and on the whole they seemed to be coming round to this solution. I wasn't going to have that, if I could help it. In my judgement Harry simply isn't tough enough to stand up to a Spanish glasshouse which would be, I suppose, really horrific. Subjected to it, he really might desert or even take his own life. The strong point for me was just this indecision of theirs. They'd never come across anything like this before and didn't really know how to cope. So I pushed hard at this weakness. Whatever they did to him, was he ever going to be any more use to them? Did they really think that punishment was going to change or reform him?

'What you don't understand, Comrade,' they said—they were very free with their 'Comrades' in speech, 'is that this Comrade is refusing to obey orders. In any army there's only one punishment for that.'

'In any capitalist army,' I corrected.

'Do you imagine Soviet Comrade soldiers can disobey orders?'

'We aren't part of the Soviet Union here—yet, Comrade. Besides, supposing the orders are silly or unjust, hasn't a Comrade any rights in the Soviet Union?'

'Orders are never silly or unjust in the Soviet Union,' Seton quite solemnly pronounced.

'It must be a very exceptional army,' I said, making a joke of it.

'It is,' Seton replied, unsmilingly.

'Anyhow,' I said, 'we are not in the Soviet Union, and this Comrade claims that he is ill. Has he seen a doctor?'

'He's been examined by a certified male nurse who can find nothing wrong.'

'He complains of stomach cramps. Have you no doctor available?'

'If we didn't think he was malingering, we would send him further back to a doctor.'

'Why not do that and test whether he is malingering or not?'

'And how do we know he wouldn't desert if we did? We can't afford the manpower to send two escorts with him.'

'If he was going to desert he would surely have deserted already, if not on the night of the engagement as the others did.'

Then we had a temporary pause while coffee was drunk and Comrade Seton began on a new tack.

'What exactly is your interest in this Comrade, Comrade Murray?'

'He was my secretary in England.'

'And was he only your secretary?'

'We worked in a democratic way together, Comrade, and it was consequently from me that he learned his Socialism. In this way I feel responsible for the situation he is in.'

'It was a curious sort of Socialism you taught him, Comrade, to teach him to refuse to obey socialist discipline.'

'We didn't think of socialist discipline as repressive discipline—that was evidently our mistake. We imagined that among Comrades the Comrades would behave reasonably.'

'What, then, is your suggestion for the treatment of this Comrade?'

'I should have thought that was obvious. He is of no use to you now. He is eating rations of which you are short and taking up time which you can't afford. He ought to be repatriated.'

The Comrade officer was shocked. 'And get off scot free?'

'In other words,' I said, 'you are more interested in punishment and making him suffer than in conducting the war as efficiently as possible?'

'It's hardly for you, Comrade, who have come here presumably for propaganda and are spending your time defending a worthless Comrade, to talk to us of efficiency.'

'As a Socialist I don't regard any human being as worthless.'

'I think I know exactly why you don't recognise the worthlessness of this particular Comrade.' The smear was obvious and I decided to attack.

'I'm not here for what you call propaganda work, Comrade. For I just don't believe in propaganda. I'm here to find

219

out the truth and write it, when I get back, as truthfully as I can. Remember that, Comrade.'

'As a Socialist, Comrade, it is your business to find out the *useful* truth and write that.'

Now, there I had them where I wanted them. I told them pretty strongly that I wasn't—never had been—interested in 'the useful truth'. But in the truth, good or bad. 'If there's inhumanity, brutality, silliness or wastefulness on our side, it's as much a part of the truth as the same thing on the other side. People have a right to know how we're behaving, as it is, not as they imagine. Make no mistake, Comrades,' I told them straight, 'I shall report exactly what I've seen and exactly what's been said. You know perfectly well that the sensible thing for you to do is to disburden yourselves of a *bouche inutile*. It's only spite and indignation—which I quite understand—that stops you. Punishing is going to do no one any good and you know it. Have some sense.'

Later

All the same arguments again round and round and round. But I think I'm winning. The hard realistic facts are that these people, though they are trying to act like what they imagine Soviet Commissars to be, haven't either the training or the tradition (thank goodness) to carry it through. Besides, they are inhibited by not being certain of their absolute powers. Clearly the Communists are (disastrously) in some danger of getting the upper hand here in Spain. But they haven't got it yet. They still have Social Democrats and even Liberals as allies and have to pay some regard to that. They daren't act as ruthlessly as they would like. After all, only a proportion even of the International Brigade are actually Communists. So they are still vulnerable to what people of liberal ideas would think, and that's where I have the advantage. I always end up every argument by reminding them that I'm going back in a day or two to report on all I have seen, including this, and they know it would look very bad if done in a certain way, in the *News Chronicle*, for instance.

I even feel rather sympathetic to them, even to the lumpish Seton. For, of course, I'm well aware that in one sense they have right absolutely on their side. Harry's behaviour is intolerable in any army, and if this were any other situation, there would be nothing to be said. But I just don't let myself think like that. I want him repatriated, and in another sense, that's reasonable, too. And I'm going to get it done. I'll have one more go at them tomorrow. And then come back once more, perhaps, before I leave. Anyhow I feel I'm wearing them down, whatever it makes them think of me; and how they're hating me!

FROM NELLIE'S DIARY

A perfectly horrid time at Albacete, except on the first day when we went up the line and that was very thrilling. The men there on the actual job were marvellous, so cheerful and brave, and making nothing of it. Just doing it and putting up with it.

Quite different when we got to the base. I suppose bases are always like this. Without the spur of action, too much time to theorise and really too little to do. It was sloppy, and morale was bad, I thought. Then we found that Pugh and Gavin had run away, no one knows where; and Seton, the same man I saw in London, was in charge—the Commissar—and was very fierce about them. 'They deserve to be shot and so they will be when we catch them,' he told me at once. I reminded him that I'd begged him to get Pugh returned before he'd really got committed, and he just brushed that aside. 'Only his extreme youth can possibly save him,' he said, 'and I doubt if it will.' Well, it seemed impossible to argue out here with the fighting only miles away, and with the battalion up on that hill facing the horrors—I actually saw the Moors in the far distance in their trenches. And it seemed as if perhaps Seton, though awful, was right.

Martin wouldn't have it. He was really extraordinary—heroic in a way. Because he had a difficult meeting with Harry, and was thoroughly disgusted with him, yet at the same time he was determined to get him sent home. He can do something I simply can't do, divide himself in two over it. He saw the Moors, too; he knows just in what way Seton has right on his side, and yet he manages not to let that interfere with his fixed intention of getting Harry out. He was terrifically tough with them and wasn't in the least put out by their accusations and sneers. And it *is* obvious that Harry's wasting their time and energy on his 'case', besides wasting food and all by being there. He ought to be punished and he ought to be sent home, and I wouldn't know which was right. Martin may feel the same, but doesn't let himself. He just goes for what he wants.

And he knows their weaknesses. 'They may be better Communists—Communists in a different sense from us—but make no mistake, they're still just a bunch of amateurs playing at soldiers and commissars. They, like us, are up against realities they've no experience for dealing with, and I should think they've probably mucked things up no end.'

We were travelling to Valencia, and all the way there Martin was very gloomy about everything. Railing against amateurism and how fatal it is. 'The other side are professional soldiers—and however inefficient professional soldiers seem to be at the beginnings of wars, they at least learn as it goes on.' He seemed to think we were losing.

Yet I can't feel we can be, not with the spirit I've seen. 'Wars are finally won not with spirit, but with arms, tanks, guns, aircraft and the knowledge of how to use them.' It's true and it frightened me. Our side do seem to be amateur—they seemed terribly amateur at Albacete. But surely there's an unconquerable spirit which can't go down, can it? When I think of those people on that train, I feel perfectly confident. On the other hand, when I think of that English group in Barcelona and their potty vindictive fighting with the other groups, I do wonder.

I'm much less happy than I was about everything. It's so easy in England to march to Hyde Park and shout and demonstrate without any awareness of the consequences of our actions. I've seen some terrible sights in the hospitals: and they all complain that they're desperately short of medical supplies, even the most essential drugs. We urge them on in the safety of England, but they have to bear the brunt. And it's terrible.

When Martin says 'amateurs' I feel the most amateur of all. I've nothing really to give except sympathy, and that isn't enough. I haven't even bothered to learn Spanish. What they need is experts, and I'm expert at absolutely nothing. After Valencia I shall go home. I, too, am a *bouche inutile*, a mère sightseer really.

FROM MARTIN'S DIARY

Valencia

The agony of this war! Of all wars, I suppose. But the special agony of this one to me is that all my passion of belief is on our side, a kind of desperate passion, too, as the odds grow against us. But my passion of pity cannot be so limited. How much easier it would be if I only had the

223

undivided passion of H . . . M . . . , an American war correspondent with whom I spent most of yesterday. He is tremendously and rightly honoured among the war correspondents, both for his unfaltering devotion to the Republican cause and his courage in getting nearer and sooner to the fighting fronts than anyone else. He talked interestingly and with relish of the Republican heroes. Not only the well-known ones like La Passionaria and El Campesino, but lesser-known ones like Kleber, Regler, Lukacz, Pacciardi, professional revolutionaries and soldiers, who have come here from all over the world to fight for the Spanish people —or anyhow for the anti-Fascist cause. He is writing a book celebrating them and dozens of others, the leaders of the Thaelmann battalion and the American, the Lincoln, and not only the leaders but the Brigaders too. He has got their histories and accounts of their extraordinary individual acts of bravery during the early fighting, when the Brigade was still untrained and disorganised and was held together at critical moments by individual toughness and heroism.

Acclimatised as he now is to the atmosphere of war, he accepts their deaths as gratefully as he does their deeds: he glories in both. To him there is only one side, ours; only one activity, fighting; and his dispatches, always in the heroic mould, have done a great deal for the Cause in America, and are widely quoted and re-published here.

It shames me to listen to him. It isn't that I don't admire inordinately this battle courage, too—something that I am all too conscious of not possessing, and which is what, after all, wars are about. But the waste, the waste! Is it guilt at my own lack of the quality that makes me flinch from his recitals, generous as I can feel them to be? Partly, I suppose. Partly, too, that I can't, like him, shut out the passion of pity. When he talks of the enemy, and the Moors especially, he talks only of black murderers. I can't see them in such simple terms. I see them as huddled, frightened,

224

indifferent foreigners, empressed into the war, torn away from their native country against their wills, or duped into coming to this cold, friendless, wind-swept country and killing only so not to be killed. The moment one sees the enemy as human, heroism and heroics seem a cruel kind of irony.

I talked to another correspondent, one who had been attached to the Franco forces earlier, and I asked him what difference he found between the two sides. He amazed me by saying 'None'; and when I pressed him—thinking surely there must be some between us who were fighting a just cause and they who patently weren't, he said:

'Yes, there is one difference. This side salute with the fist clenched—so; the other salutes with the arm straight out—so.'

The truth behind this, the amount of truth behind it, if it isn't the whole truth, is just what inhibits me from being able to exult like H . . . M . . . in his heroes. But I wish I could. How much easier it would be, and how necessary it is, too, since after all it's that spirit, not mine, that wins battles.

The more I hear of it, the more I hate this war. Yet I can't, like Harry, adopt a purely pacifist position. If ever a war had to be fought, it is this one. If ever a group of people were united in their wish to throw off oppression and control their own lives, it is these people. The simple faith in the justice of their cause that you meet everywhere is humbling. My own inability to stand with the heroes even in spirit, let alone the flesh, is humiliating. I am simply torn into pieces by the division in myself and feel I shall never recover. And what am I primarily doing here, anyhow, but worrying myself sick about the life of one, from this point of view equally useless, life, when so many thousand useful ones are lost every day? It is difficult to persuade myself after a day spent among the corre-

225

spondents that what I am doing has to be done. Yet I cling to it as about the one thing I am capable of doing in the whole of this full-scale horror. And if I didn't do the one thing I can do to prevent just one wholly unimportant but unnecessary death, I should, I know, somehow betray myself.

FROM NELLIE'S DIARY

Valencia

I must put this all down while it is quite fresh in my mind, partly because I must broadcast and try and write an article about the atrocity itself: partly because it confirmed all too clearly in my mind what Martin has been saying:

IN A WAR THERE'S NO ROOM FOR AMATEURS.

It's too serious for that.

Not that they were all hopeless. The hospitals, schools and settlements they took me to on the way South seemed fairly well run. We were on a tour down South from Valencia. There isn't quite the same gaiety and spontanaiety that I so loved in Barcelona. Things are grimmer. There's no doubt about that. The war isn't going so well. You can feel it everywhere in the atmosphere. The German Air Force has pretty well complete domination of the air, and they say that there are more and more Italian troops landing. Unless England and France do something, it's going to be very grave. That's what they all say, and it must be true. I suppose the Russians are helping with arms. But not with troops and aircraft. You never see any Russians here.

Anyhow, down we drove, stopping at various places to visit, and got to Almeria about tea-time; and we noticed at once that the place was crowded. Thousands of women in bedraggled black, surrounded by children everywhere on the pavements in a state of dazed bewilderment. They flowed all over the squares and streets, and we had to nose our way through. My interpreter and driver—a rather sour woman actually—stopped and tried to find out what was happening. The rumour was that Malaga, to which we were supposed to be going, had been captured by the Italians who were driving up the coast, and these were refugees coming in ahead of them.

My interpreter said there were always these rumours, and we should take no notice and drive on. So we pushed our way through and out on to the Malaga road; and all along by the side of it, there was this unending trail of women in black, carrying a few household possessions and the children dragging by their side. They stumbled along, shuffling through the dust and moaning so that there seemed to be a continual cry of 'Aiee! Aiee!' rising from them. Then coming past them in single file what must have been a whole regiment of militia-men with their rifles slung, a bedraggled army in retreat.

We had to go very slowly: it took us more than an hour to go eight miles; and all the time with this sad procession dragging past. Then we came to a long hill, and looked down, and there as far as the eye could see, miles and miles of this winding black mass, shuffling wearily along. Miles and miles.

We stopped there in sheer amazement. There wasn't any doubt about it now. Malaga had fallen and these were refugees crowding into Almeria, which couldn't cope with what it had got already. Then a terrible thing happened. A plane droned overhead, and the whole long stream as far as one could see scattered to the side and lay down, so that suddenly the long dusty road was empty again, and we the only people on it. They must have already been bombed or machine-gunned, they knew so well what to do. The plane passed, and they rose again like black ghosts, and the treck began again, the long shuffle towards what they imagined was safety.

There was no point in our going on. My interpreter seemed simply dazed, but I insisted we go back to Almeria and try to get them to organise something there. They couldn't have any idea how many thousands were going to pass into the little town by nightfall. They must be put on their guard to get something ready. She agreed, and we turned the car round, and immediately we were in the centre of a fighting mob trying to get in. We could only squeeze in five, an old woman, a nursing mother and her baby, one woman who seemed to have been wounded in the arm and her two little boys. But we couldn't get away at first, we were surrounded by misery, women showing their blistered feet, women begging us to take their children, women shouting, screaming, cursing. Then one of them lifted up her black skirt there in the road and showed her belly round with child. I got out and gave her my place. It was the least I could do. I told my interpreter I'd be all right. I'd make my way to the Communist headquarters and find her there; and gradually she pushed her way through the pleading women and got started. I told her to try and get a convoy of trucks out to pick up the sick and wounded. But she never did. She drove off and I was left on the road.

It was even more pitiful at close quarters. I couldn't understand more than a few words of Spanish but I soon gathered from their descriptive gestures what had happenned. Malaga was in flames, and the Fascists were coming up the road. They'd been machine-gunned by planes—and they made graphic sounds of bullets tearing up the road. And they interspersed it all with their cry of 'Aiee! Aiee!', as they shuffled on up the road. Night began to fall, and another plane was heard and they pulled me into the side
228

and threw me down, and sure enough this one drove up the road spraying it with bullets, and we crouched and shouted.

Could anything have been more barbaric than trying to mow down these wretched defenceless women? What was the point except sheer terrorization? And I found myself impotently shaking my fist at the sky after they had gone. Useless, vain gesture.

It was a horrible three hours. I hate walking, and my heels were too high. But I was glad to be doing it, to be sharing just that much with these poor victims of the war. No slipping off for a waiting taxi.

Here we trudged and shuffled along ceaselessly moaning and crying. Everyone talked in a whisper, as if a loud voice might attract another enemy plane. But every now and then a child would be lost and an anguished cry of 'Maria' or 'Pepe' would ring out. There seemed to be ever so many children without their parents, just wandering along in a sort of semi-daze. I collected half a dozen and we formed a chain: they were so trusting, their hot little hands linked with mine, just gratified to find someone they could cling to.

There was a dark velvet night sky, it was warm luckily, and on we trudged and I felt (I wonder if anyone will understand this) curiously responsible. Of course we didn't will this, when we marched in England, egging the Spanish on, we didn't will this drift of women. But we didn't, either, take into account that this was what our meetings and messages of encouragement had flowered into, this poor black blank procession of the defeated. If we're going to encourage people to resist in future, I found myself thinking, we've got to take this into account and cope with it, for God's sake. I don't know. I just felt that I and everyone at home bears some responsibility for it. How are they to be fed, cared for, bedded, this enormous number? Who'd do anything for them? On they shuffle, as if they hope to find something to relieve them. But is there anything for them in that overcrowded town?

'Aiee! Aiee!' I was soon moaning it, too, moaning it with the rest when I wasn't trying to cheer up my little band of children. They were so sleepy, too. One little girl on the outside let go and she simply spun, toppled and fell where she was—fast asleep. We tried to wake her but we couldn't. I tried to carry her, but I soon saw I shouldn't be able to—not even that. We left her lying there by the side of the road. What would happen to her?

I crawled into Almeria more dead than alive, my feet in a terrible state. The confusion there was beyond anything I can describe. The whole place simply swamped with these refugees sprawled over every empty space and sitting hopelessly, patiently, waiting for something to be done for them, and nothing was being done at all. I made my way at last to the Communist Party Headquarters and found them under heavy guard, keeping the refugees out. There were about twenty men with rifles, and if the women came and asked anything, they just shoved them away. My interpreter was there and I asked what they were doing about it, and she just shrugged her shoulders and said, 'What could they do?' They'd telegraphed to Murcia, the provincial capital, for supplies, and they'd probably come in a day or two. *A day or two*! But what were they doing meanwhile, I said. There was nothing *to* do, she said. But I had noticed all the houses in the town were barred and shuttered. Why didn't they go out and get them opened up, share out the food, blankets, beds—get the children in, if no one else. But she just shrugged her shoulders.

They'd simply given up, and were doing nothing, nothing at all. This headquarters was a large building and almost empty. There were some women helpers in the kitchen solemnly frying eggs, slowly one by one, and eating them themselves or sending them out to the guards to munch in front of all those starving, exhausted people. I was *furious*. I had brought my five orphans along with me and deposited them outside and was determined to do something for them, if for no one else. So I explored the upstairs of the building and found four dormitories with beds in each—they belonged to the guards and the women, I suppose. So I marched down into the kitchen and had another look there. I could see that I wasn't popular, but I was past caring about that. There were large cans of milk and a lot of bread.

I brought my children in, and got hold of four of the guards lounging at the door and shouted at them, 'Los Ninos, Los Ninos!' And they do respond to that—the Spanish. With a lot of gesturing, I showed them what I wanted, and we soon pushed the egg-frying women aside and got four great pans of milk steaming on the stoves and broke the bread up into it. Then with my four more or less reluctant helpers I went out and collected all the kids in sight, about a hundred, I suppose, prized them away from their mothers and fed them the bread and milk inside. The women were protesting, but I brushed them aside, and after the meal I took the children upstairs, the whole lot, and packed them into the beds—the whole lot, four to a bed! And they snuggled over and went to sleep. I thought this example might fire the others to do something for the rest of the people out there. But they just refused to understand when I tried to explain, and muttered in corners.

I didn't care. I'd done what I could, and I was exhausted. I went up and slept on a bench in one of the passages guarding the dormitories.

Then suddenly I was woken by this fearful crash. We were being bombed. That wretched town crammed with refugees was actually being bombed! My troop of children set up a terrible hullaballo of weeping and crying, and I rushed from room to room comforting and quietening. I don't know how many bombs there were—not so many—a dozen perhaps, but the terror it caused in the crowded town! Our building wasn't hit, mercifully, But several fires were raging, fire engines clanged, and those poor women outside set up a dismal howl. It was unimaginable.

There was nothing I could do except go on comforting my children, till, at last, the women outside fell silent again, the fires died down, and a sort of ghastly peace descended once more.

I couldn't get to sleep myself. I don't know whether I was more outraged by this further act of barbaric terrorization, or by the incompetence that had left all these women and children at the mercy of this horror. Something should have been done. It should have been foreseen. They were all helpless amateurs, and I myself as bad as any of them. What was I doing here, if I couldn't have taken the trouble to learn enough Spanish to get something done myself?

The next morning I got up early and went down to the kitchen to make more bread-and-milk for my children, and I found everyone in a very hostile mood. My four helpers of the night before wouldn't help, and the women jabbered at me angrily in Spanish I didn't understand. But they didn't actually interfere. I think they saw I wasn't in a mood to be interfered with. And I got my children down and ladled them out their breakfast.

Then my interpreter arrived and told me she had strict orders to leave at once. The authorities now had things in hand: supplies were coming from Murcia. They didn't want extra mouths hanging round, and we were to leave immediately. I didn't really believe her. But I didn't see what more I could do, so I agreed to go, though it cost a pang leaving my poor orphans.

I shall make one more broadcast and then go back to England. My broadcast will be about the refugees, the machine-gunning and the bombing—not all the rest. I've learned that lesson from Martin, to learn to keep things separate in one's mind.

The inefficiency and lack of preparedness is something I've got to think about. I haven't got it all clear but it links up in my mind with this feeling of guilt, of a responsibility we haven't any of us really taken. I don't quite know what I mean but I do know that if I could have foreseen what happened on that road and in that town, I shouldn't have been so smug and certain, as I was in England. Can't get it any clearer for the moment.

FROM MARTIN'S DIARY

Valencia

Been very busy lecturing, broadcasting, interviewing, sending back articles, etc. Don't know how much good it does. But it does seem to be welcome. With the two Democracies holding back and doing nothing to help and a lot to hinder, the Spaniards here feel deserted and friendless. Any sign that they have friends and allies outside is something, though not, of course, very much. Their constant plea, can't we get England and France to help actively? Perhaps I should be better at home trying to do that. Only I know it's hopeless. The iron ring is closing in, and this marvellous upsurge of freedom is going to be strangled to death. It's inevitable. I know it now, and it's too pitiful to think of. Wystan's superb poem said it all:

The stars are dead: the animals will not look.
We are left alone with our day and the time is short and History to the defeated
May say Alas, but cannot help nor pardon.

Here in Valencia there are air-raid alarms every night.

Malaga has fallen to a new influx of Italian troops. Nellie who arrived today, was in on it and gave a very good broadcast about it. Will it move anyone but us? Nellie was in a strange mood. Something has happened to her. She described the inefficiency at Almeria and I can just imagine her in her most formidable upper-class manner taking charge. But it's changed her. She was more silent than usual and thoughtful, and most amazing of all, talked, too, as if the end was inevitable. Quite different from her early days here. The experience must have been even more horrifying than she lets on; and her romanticism seems to have received a mortal blow. She is cutting short her stay and going back tomorrow. I shan't stay much longer myself either. I shall make one more visit to Albacete and, if I can, to Madrid, then back.

Later

We found the boys tonight! There was the usual air-raid warning, and down in the shelter I suddenly spotted Gavin, and Pugh with him. They were on leave from the Teruel front, where they had joined up with a Spanish militia battalion, and were in the highest of high spirits and couldn't understand why anyone had been worried about them. They'd left Albacete as they had said they would. There was a young Spanish Captain on leave there who'd had an affair with Pugh, and had learned of their predicament, confined to base. He had simply said, 'Why not come along back with me? We need people like you.' So they had. They'd gone with him to the Teruel front and just joined in with the militia fighting there. 'So we aren't deserters at all,' they said. 'On the contrary we've exchanged our typewriters for rifles. There can't be anything culpable about that.' 'You should hear what they say about you in Albacete,' I told them, but they only laughed. They regarded Commissar Seton as a good joke, and said that no one took

234

him seriously. Besides, the English were very unpopular in Spain owing to our Government's indifference.

When the raid ended we went up and had dinner together and I've never known Gavin so gay. Pugh was just as usual. I simply couldn't make Gavin out at all. Who would have thought that he, of all people, would at last have found whatever satisfaction he was seeking in the firing line? He didn't seem to think it needed explaining. Fighting, he said, was only a small part of the experience. It was only rarely that things got dangerous. Most of the time it had been a pretty quiescent front and it was very well organised. Their's was a Socialist Militia. They were only up in the line half the time and half in reserve. 'It's pretty boring, really, isn't it, Pugh? But we manage to have fun, don't we?'

Yet if it was boring, it was obviously boring in a quite different sense from London. Is it that he gets some deep satisfaction from finding that he can stick it? Did he feel before that his brother Spencer was the one who did everything, and he's now on terms with him? Impossible to say. He just seems to have found a place where he no longer is filled with anxieties and doubts. Of course a line-soldier's life, once you accept the danger, is totally free from any responsibilities or problems. Perhaps that's what's done the trick for him. Whatever it is, it's worked a sort of miracle and I've never seen him so happy and carefree.

You would expect that with Pugh, of course. What surprised me was that Nellie afterwards was absolutely reconciled to Pugh being there. She said, 'I see that all my fears and anxieties about him were neurotic. I suppose they were about me, not him. He's perfectly at one with himself, isn't he?' And that was the impression he gave. He was having the time of his life. But that Nellie should see it, and accept it, is another sort of miracle. I would never myself have doubted Pugh's ability to find the life enjoyable, but Gavin? Far the most educated, civilised and sybaritic of the three. You'd have thought all the conditions militated against his putting up with it, the people, the danger, the active discomfort, the lack of distractions. . . . And how, I wonder, will it work for the future? I see that Pugh when he gets back—one somehow assumes that the Pughs of this world do get back—will simply find another similar outlet. But how will Gavin cope later, with his mother and Oxford and London? For that very reason one wonders with him, if he ever will have to.

Finally, full of spirits, they went off to some party in the flat of a Duc they've linked up with. They wanted us to go too. But neither of us felt like that sort of thing in the Spain of the moment.

Later. Madrid

Madrid! Has there ever been anything like Madrid, ringed round by the enemy except for one narrow road out, yet holding on and more than holding on? Life goes on in the capital, not quite as if none of this was happening, but at least as if it shall interfere as little as possible with the daily routine of living. It's no longer being bombed as it was at the beginning—and everywhere there's the evidence of this vicious bombing in the torn-down houses and the gaps in the façades. But every so often a shell comes bursting into the city. The enemy have one big gun trained on it: and at regular intervals the shell from it drops in. It's most uncanny this regularity. As it comes in people look at their watches and remark, 'It's late today,' and that's all the notice taken except by those who happen to be hit; and ambulances scream up and the corpses and the debris are cleared away. Otherwise life goes on, with the perpetual sound of gunfire out at the University City where the front is still active.

I am housed in a mansion put aside for correspondents and 'cultural visitors'. It is kept up exactly as it was before the war except that the more valuable pictures and objects have been removed to safety. But even with these gone the house has an air of decayed splendour in contrast to the shabby city outside. There are said to be many fifth column-ists still about in the city, and often at night there is a tearing of cars and a wild burst of shooting that no one talks about afterwards. The food is poor and not much of it. No coffee, but some foul sort of brandy that we drink after our com-munal meal in the basement. Morale here is amazingly high in spite of everything, higher perhaps than anywhere else except Barcelona. All the officials I talked to were con-fident and assured. I never heard the possibility of defeat even hinted at. But the correspondents are not so optimistic.

I was taken out to University City on the outskirts of the town, an experience so bizarre it is difficult to describe. The front lines were two buildings opposite each other, the buildings now pockmarked with bullets or ravaged with shells. But somehow each side had settled into its own building, and there they were locked together at a distance only of a wide street. Every so often the buildings would errupt into rifle-fire and then it would die down again into sniping.

A touching thing. Because they were in a University, the Republican soldiers were learning to read and write, and this front-line post of theirs was also a sort of classroom with alphabets and charts spread out and pinned up. This is to me symbolic of the whole of this war. What saved the Republic at the outset and what keeps them going in spite of the odds against them is the untutored conviction of the mass of ordinary simple people that it is better to die in freedom than submit to tyranny all their lives. They have been tyran-nized by the bosses, the absentee landlords and, above all, the Church. So much so that illiteracy was the common thing among the working masses. The Republic, for all its faults, gave them a glimpse of a better life and they have responded to that hope everywhere. They are fighting be-

237

cause they want to defend the first taste of liberty they have had for centuries, and the Fascists would take that away from them. I know just what Nellie means by saying that such a spirit is unconquerable, but, alas, that is only a metaphor, and metaphors can be blown to smithereens by bombs and shells and machine-guns. And it has become a question no longer of Right or Wrong, Justice or Injustice, but of which side can get hold of the larger accumulation of the means of killing. And with England and France refusing their aid, can the Republic in the end fail to be strangled? And that it is its fellow Democracies who are strangling it, is a ghastly irony. The weakness of our National Government in the face of the Dictators! Allowing Hitler and Mussolini to pour in arms and men and to sink ships in the Mediterranean, isn't, either, just an exacerbation of this 'local trouble' as they like to think of it. If we can't resist them in this clear case, how shall we stand up to their next demands?

Later. Albacete

Nellie left. I've come here for a last round with Comrade Commissar Seton. Harry as tiresome and obstinate as ever. Comrade Seton, though, giving ground I thought. While I was about it, I raised the question of Gavin and Pugh but found him very adamant on that. I didn't like to admit having seen them in case they should be traced, and clearly Seton, if he was relaxing a bit over Harry, was making it up by being extra ferocious about the other two.

Actually, before I left Valencia I had an interview with the Socialist Minister who had asked me to lunch, and found him so sympathetic that I told him about the two boys. The idea of their 'deserting' from a base in order to fight tickled him immensely, and he took all the particulars and promised to see they were protected, as far as he could. Although he tried to cover it up, I could see that he was very gloomy

238

about the war. Here, at Albacete, they seem to have no idea what's really going on, or to have blinkered themselves against it. I made a mistake in coming here first. This little closed Communist enclave isn't Spain or what the war's about. After being round so much I see it now for what it is—a little piece of provincial England stuck down here. It's had a sort of propaganda use—International help, etc.— but that's about all.

Typically, when I introduced the subject of Gavin and Pugh and gave as a hypothesis that they might have run away in order to get into a fighting unit, Seton said it was highly unlikely, and I said, 'Not at all. I know these boys and what they were like.'

'You know too many boys for your own good,' was Seton's way of scoring. Well, I suppose that's what you'd expect from provincial England. But my guess is that Harry will be repatriated quite soon all the same.

Later. London

I left Spain yesterday and found the old world where I left it, full of shabby excuses for inaction, and a wilful turning of the blind eye to the tragedy of Spain. It has all the marks—Spain—of a tragedy, in which Greatness is not enough to conquer and to be Right is not necessarily to win. The Spanish people have been heroic in their immediate and, as it were, instinctive response to the attempt to rob them of their freedom: and as you meet them in the cafés or lorries, as drivers and soldiers, they strike one still as heroic. They are so confident in their own strength and their ability to withstand their oppressors, and they express it with a touching simplicity.

If life were only as simple as they are! And I don't mean simple in any derogatory sense. Their response, the response of the average Spanish worker, is wholly uncomplicated. 'We've got to win or die in the attempt.' But how are they to know of the machinations of the Communists, of the pressures put on the Government by the Russians, or the seedy struggle for power that is going on with growing intensity in the Ministries?

I had many sidelights on this, and it is almost impossible to reconcile, after being so close to it all, the uncalculating courage and sacrifice of the masses with the devious and complicated manoeuvring of the politicians. Yet I, if anyone should know that there is nothing simple about the issues. I who have been engaged in a sideline warfare over one individual and his future. In England before we came here the issues looked so crystal clear, simple Right against simple Wrong. But, of course, no human issues are as simple as that in reality. History will have another and far more complex account of it all. After all, on the personal plane I have set myself to defend a position that is 'really' indefensible. Only what does 'really' mean? I can defend my position and do, and fight for it, and even believe that I have won. Yet it isn't a victory I can be very proud of.

What one has to have is a charity that is almost beyond human possibility. Thus if we are fully human we must accept that the other side, too, has its heroes—Spain is a land of heroics—that they too have a Cause that they are prepared to die for—they are not all conscripts: that they, too, suffer and die in pain. If Madrid was 'martyred' by the Fascist bombs, so too, no doubt, was Seville by ours. We are fiercely indignant when children are blown to pieces in the streets of Almeria, but children are blown to pieces in their streets, too.

Yet this can't lead to the simple conclusion that all war is condemnable. It is damnable, but that is another thing. This one had to be fought. Even the most pacifist-minded of the Left would surely subscribe to that. It had to be fought, even if, as I'm coming to think, it can't be won. And that's another contradiction that one must

240

sustain with all the charity that one can command. Only a great poet could express the myriad contradictions that this struggle throws up.

Now that I've got back to England, what am I to do? Still, I think, do all I can in the way of propaganda to sustain the Spanish people, even though I feel it to be hopeless? Should I stifle such doubts and go on as if they weren't there, helping to prolong the agony? Yes, surely as long as there is the slightest chance that the position can be reversed. Yet it will be a weary business, stirring up the faithful and the already converted—keeping their hopes up—when the only thing that really matters is converting the unconverted, the Government that is, who aren't going to listen to me, or my sort.

What the Communists would say is that what I call stirring up the faithful is really an act of essential political education. A Communist is lucky in that he isn't concerned, doesn't give a fuck, for the deaths of the innocent or even for the rights and the wrongs. To him the Spanish struggle is simply a useful occasion, another chance to work up indignation and spread the gospel. He would keep it going long beyond what is sensible even, in order to have this propaganda material under his belt. The Communists are not really interested in Spain as such or the Spanish struggle as such.

They are interested only in the USSR and its influence in the world. If Franco aims to turn Spain into a Fascist sphere of influence, the Communists aim to turn it into a Soviet one. Yet in England I shall find that it is the Communists who are at the forefront of all the demonstrations and meetings on behalf of the Republic, and it is under their aegis that I shall be speaking and writing.

Yet having seen what I have seen and experienced what I have experienced, I couldn't not, at the least, bear witness to this heroism in England, even if it has to be done under the aegis of the Communists. Another contradiction, another irreconcilable to be reconciled somehow. And in the end one reconciles oneself to it by convincing oneself that however complex the issues are, however muddled with irreconcilables, our cause is Just and theirs is not. Freedom is more important than order, and the fraternity that this has engendered among the ordinary Spanish people is a value that is worth fighting for. Even if the Communists don't really themselves believe in freedom, the circumstances compel them to preach it, and the lesson may get home. I can convince myself, too, that it is worth hammering at the Ruling Classes, to try even at this late date to convince them that the appetite of the Dictators is insatiable, and that sooner rather than later they must be resisted. If not, surely the whole of Europe will suffer what the Spanish people are now enduring.

PART SIX

Conclusion

Nellie was the first of the party to get back and the change in her was immediately noticeable. In earlier days she had been wholly confident in her beliefs, however muddled her expression of them. But now she was in a state of political confusion. Her admiration for the Spanish masses remained complete. From the notes I made of her conversations at the time I see that she would return again and again to the impact made on her by her first glimpse of Anarchist Barcelona, and of how she found a similar marvellous sense of discovered freedom among all the ordinary people she came across. What dismayed her was the realisation that this was not enough to win the war. She was to suffer the painful death of her romanticism all through the agony of the last months of the Republic.

And then she had to face—and found it very hard—the unwelcome fact that Communism in action was something very different from Communism in theory. In this she was not, of course, unique. Thousands of radical intellectuals in this decade endured a similar painful disillusion as they saw their liberal optimism founder on the reef of Soviet realism. Perhaps something of the sort is an inevitable part of growing up. Perhaps the young people of today who hopefully march through the streets chanting Ho! Ho! Ho Chi Minh! will have to discover in their turn—and no less painfully—that a tyrant is a tyrant and that tyranny is not, in practice, an endurable state for anyone accustomed to freedom.

But Nellie was, whatever she was not, immensely resilient. She soon had what her brother David called 'a new bee in her bonnet'. She was now convinced in a more vivid and more practical sense that War was coming, and that Hitler and Mussolini had been only practising for that in Spain. And knowing now something of what war actually looked like at close quarters, she began badgering David about the Government's preparations against that event. David was, as one would have expected, a Chamberlainite, and his head was pretty deeply buried in the sand of that particular optimism; and he was acutely embarrassed by a new Nellie who forced herself on him socially in order to pester the high-ups she met with him about the necessity for facing the truth.

Then her new obsession took a practical turn. What preparations were being made to cope with civilian casualties in the devastating air-raids which were then expected (for hadn't Baldwin pronounced that the bomber would always get through?) And she now shamelessly used her title to get herself in at the top of the Red Cross and stir them there into preparatory action.

She had already dropped the Bookshop crowd and had positively decided never again to appear on a Communist platform, and gradually she was to drop out of our circle.

Martin arrived about a week later and he, too, was in a state of painful political indecision. He had had a particularly upsetting series of interviews before he left. The situation of the Republic was deteriorating rapidly and, worse, in the internecine struggles within the Government, the Communists were gaining the upper hand, for the Russians were making it a condition of continuing to supply arms that the Party should have an increased share of power. Worse again, there was definite evidence that the Soviet Secret Police had arrived in Spain, and had already liquidated a number of Anarchists and Socialists.

What worried him was whether it was right to continue to pretend that all was well and to lend his public support to the rallies and demonstrations which were still going on in full strength in England under the Communist influen_{ce}. Oughtn't he to tell the truth as he knew it, however unpopular it might be? Again, the war was now clearly lost: was it, then, really in the best interests of the Spanish people to encourage them to continue it to the bitter end? The Communists, of course, had no doubts about it. But their attitude was now to him wholly suspect. They weren't thinking of the Spanish people, and never had. To them the war had been a very important means of political education and recruitment, and they wouldn't hesitate to prolong it so long as it was still serving those ends. But oughtn't some sort of peace formula to be found while there were still so many lives to be saved?

To have said anything of the sort in public at this time would have been regarded as the worst kind of treachery; for all the propaganda put out in England—and there was a great deal of it—obscured the real political issues and still gave the Republic a fighting chance.

Martin compromised in the end by making his real views known in private conversations and interviews, while in public dwelling on the heroic nature of the Spanish people. He never mentioned the English battalion. The one bright spot for him was that a week after his own arrival, Harry turned up, 'repatriated for medical reasons'.

It would have been at about this time, too, that we learned that Pugh had been 'shot'. There was no explanation of any kind, but the report was from a usually reliable correspondent. We speculated a good deal about this. The expression 'shot' certainly suggested that he wasn't an ordinary war casualty. Nellie's brother naturally tried, through diplomatic channels, to get some explanation, but none was forthcoming.

Nor could Gavin, when he arrived a week or two later, throw much light on it. He and Pugh had, it seemed, been seeing a good deal of that Duc whom they had mentioned to Martin and Nellie in Valencia. This man, whom Gavin

247

suspected of being a fifth columnist, had a grand apartment in Valencia and was lavish with food and, especially, drink. And a lot of poker was played.

Gavin, who had never been addicted either to drink or to gambling, accompanied Pugh there less and less, until one day he was picked up by the military police in the street and carted off to jail. He naturally imagined that his 'desertion' from the International Brigade would now come out and that he would be sent back to Albacete to face the music. Instead of that, he was suddenly told he was to be repatriated, was released and put on a train for England. He never made clear to me—perhaps he had never made it clear to himself—what it was about his spell on the Teruel front that had seemed to satisfy him. He dodged the subject when I brought it up.

As for Pugh, Gavin only added that the police might easily have been on to the Duc and he was sure that, if they had arrived, Pugh would have done his best to get away, so might easily have been shot 'while resisting arrest'.

It was certainly an odd irony that of those of us who went to Spain, Pugh, the least committed of all, was the only one to be killed there.

Our group rather split up in the next year or two, but the last agonies of the Spanish Republic were something that we were all mourning when we did see each other. It seemed, as indeed it was, the end of an era for us, politically speaking. We had all felt that the Spanish people simply could not be defeated, and to discover that justice had so little to do with results was a mortal blow to our political romanticism. Meanwhile there was now Munich and Czechoslovakia to agonise over.

But something had gone out of our enthusiasm; or rather, perhaps, we had come to realise how futile and impotent angry gestures were in the face of overwhelming force. No amount of demonstrating or speech-making was

248

going to deter Chamberlain and Horace Wilson from their determination to sell the Czechs down the river, and none of us joined in the demos of this period. We watched the war coming with a kind of deadened anticipation and accepted it dully when it came.

Martin married Elvira and spent most of the intervening time abroad with occasional visits home. Harry joined the Quakers and several other bodies of the same kind, and went off to do some sort of relief work in the provinces. Gavin, through the influence of his uncle, was accepted back at Oxford, but even being something of a hero didn't reconcile him to the place.

When the war did come he joined the Guards and was captured in the retreat to Dunkirk; but I don't myself think that it was his long imprisonment which was entirely responsible for his subsequently committing suicide. Wasn't he always heading that way?

Harry signed up as a conscientious objector and was exempted. Martin came back and went into the Ministry of Information. Nellie came into her own high up in the Red Cross. I myself joined the Air Force as an intelligence officer.

Then, as a postscript, I heard in the middle of the war the true account of Pugh's death. I met a journalist who was in Valencia at that time. It was more or less as Gavin had suspected. The Duc with the grand flat was indeed a fifth columnist. Pugh had had enough of fighting, and the Duc had promised to hide him until the Falangists arrived. This journalist had seen a good deal of them: they were more often drunk than sober. As the Franco forces closed in on Valencia, too, the security forces tightened their net: the Duc and Pugh were rounded up, and shot out of hand.